WHAT YOUR BROKER NEVER TELLS YOU

WHAT YOUR BROKER NEVER TELLS YOU

A guide to becoming a better player

R. Andrew Groth

Published And Distributed By
M/T MARKETING GROUP
Michigan / California

All rights reserved.
Copyright 1994 by R. Andrew Groth
Revised 1997

Library of Congress Catalog Card No: 97-93043
ISBN 0-9656976-0-6

For more information contact:
M/T Marketing Group, Inc.
5983 Pleasant Dr. Suite 1000
P.O. Box 300263
Drayton Plains, MI 48330-0263

Phone: (TOLL FREE) 1-888-219-2748
E-Mail: mtmarketing@juno.com
WEB Site: www.mtmarketing.com

Printed in the United States of America

THIS BOOK IS
DEDICATED TO MY
GRANDFATHER

ANDREW NAGY
1902-1994

CONTENTS

Page

III   Acknowledgments

V   Preface

1   Chapter 1   YOUR BROKER
Friend, Foe, or Both?...

27   Chapter 2   THE BROKERAGE HOUSE
Whose Money Is It, Anyway?...

41   Chapter 3   INVESTMENT PRODUCTS
A Great Place For Commissions To Hide...

61   Chapter 4   RESEARCH ANALYSTS
Gurus or Gophers?...

77   Chapter 5   MANAGED ACCOUNTS
The Fairest Game In Town...

93   Chapter 6   QUESTIONS YOU MAY WANT TO ASK...

117   Glossary

ACKNOWLEDGMENTS

To my wife, Bev: who never stopped believing in me and whose presence in my life brings indescribable joy…

Special thanks to Mario Cotruvo:
who's creative talent was invaluable…

President, Cotruvo & Associates
San Rafael, CA

PREFACE

After ten years as a stockbroker and Vice President for two of Wall Street's largest firms and having owned my own business for eight years, the time had come to reflect on the investment process. The catalyst that prompted me to begin this undertaking was, of all things, a billboard I saw along a Detroit freeway. The message: "**Trust in God, but First Cut the Cards**". It made me smile because of its amusing philosophy and its application to my work. While this cynical advice is useful in any financial transaction you may enter, it has special meaning if you are an investor using the services of a stockbroker.

I have tackled this project from the perspective of the investment advisor as well as the client. In retrospect, it became *painfully* obvious that their objectives were not always the same. The client usually believed that his* goals were also that of his broker, when - in reality - the advisor had his own agenda. When the goals did coincide it was usually because both parties' interests were served.

Let me be clear from the outset that the focus of this book is not **"*broker bashing*".** Most brokers serving the public are trustworthy and try to do their best for their clients. But let me also make clear that there is a nagging and inherent conflict of interest between the broker and his client that will be discussed at length in the first chapter. Most of us are aware that every profession has its bad apples - attorneys, teachers, dentists, life insurance salespeople, etc. So, rather

(Whenever the neuter is not used in this book, the masculine gender is employed for convenience purposes only. It has no other implications, implied or otherwise.)

WHAT YOUR BROKER NEVER TELLS YOU

than discuss *"bad brokers"*, this book is intended to help you, the investor, understand the "game". "**What?** you say **GAME?**" Indeed it is! And in order to *"win"* - that is, increase the number of chips you have - it is imperative that you understand the "**rules**". For example, can you imagine stepping into the batter's box when it's your turn to bat and not knowing how many ball and strikes you're entitled to? It's virtually impossible to win any game when you're in the dark about how the rules govern the outcome. In terms of investing, I'm not just referring to economic rules, such as price/earnings ratios, market timing, yield curve analysis, asset allocation, etc. I'm also talking about understanding the players you're dealing with: your broker, the brokerage house, in-house analysts - and all of their respective agendas so that the playing field is leveled.

If you assume, even for a moment, that your broker and the brokerage house are interested solely in your financial welfare, cash in your chips now! In a perfect world, this would be true. This book is not interested in **"oughta be's"**, but only in the *"what is"*. In his best-selling book **MILLION DOLLAR HABITS**, author Robert Ringer states:

> "…most people live an a totally unreal world. They create a world in their own minds based on the way they would like the world to be rather than the way it actually is."

He further states,

> "A faulty perception of reality is almost always destructive, sometimes fatal."

WHAT YOUR BROKER NEVER TELLS YOU

In understanding the way things are - rather than the way you would like them to be - you will not only be more confident in the long run but you will probably increase the odds of multiplying the number of chips in your pile.

A final note: this book is based on my real life experiences in the brokerage business. It is what I lived through everyday for ten years. While my conclusions are my own opinions, I believe they fairly represent the industry. If your broker is everything you hoped for and more - fantastic! My goal is not to create acrimony and mistrust, but simply to make the transactions less one-sided - to **your** benefit.

If you come across terms unfamiliar to you, check the glossary at the back of the book for clarification.

That being said, are you ready to become a better **player**? Good! Then let's begin to see how the game is played…

CHAPTER ONE
YOUR BROKER

Friend, Foe or Both?...

CHAPTER ONE

Let me reiterate: I am *not* interested in maligning your broker. He may be an exemplary person - quite possibly your friend. I saw a broker financially devastate his life long friend for the sake of commissions. Friendship is irrelevant, so let's set aside any emotional involvement. It's time to look at the fundamentals and how the system works. This illustration may help put the process in a clearer light: *See Fig. 1*

Before you can even *begin* to make money, as seen in the illustration, you need to be mindful that two groups of people have an eye on your chips. Remember: your money is *ALWAYS* up for grabs; thus, when you decide to invest your funds with a full-service broker, it's vital to know how the commissions are paid and who is getting paid what amount. One alternative is to use a discount broker. We will discuss this option in a later chapter.

Here are several **critically** important rules to keep in mind as you begin to play the game:

RULE #1

Remember that brokers are paid virtually every time money is invested. There's nothing wrong with that - it's the American Way, but you must learn how to keep him honest. In

WHAT YOUR BROKER NEVER TELLS YOU

Figure 1

WHAT YOUR BROKER NEVER TELLS YOU

virtually every stock transaction, for example, there is a *"round trip"* commission, meaning that your broker gets his cut on the buy **AS WELL AS** the sell side - even if you have lost money on the trade. I remember many dismayed clients complaining of paying a commission when they sold at a loss. They wrongfully assumed that I would only charge them a commission on the sell side if they MADE money. Wrong! Whether they made money or not, I *ALWAYS* got paid! Friends of mine outside the business used to laugh, saying I reminded them of a "bookie" because I got paid regardless of the outcome. It figures, then, that if your broker gets paid every time he moves your money, he is highly motivated to do so on a consistent basis if he intends to make a substantial living. Sometimes, when we were "light" on commissions, we would look for ways to move money around. I'm embarrassed to say that we laughingly referred to this persistent rearranging of clients money as *"portfolio adjustments"*. It isn't a coincidence that this procedure usually happened at the end of the month. One broker I knew was so creative at generating commissions that he routinely sold naked puts - IN PENSION PLANS! For those unfamiliar with this strategy, you need to grasp two very important points:

- Your risk is UNLIMITED with this strategy.

- It is illegal (in most plans) and certainly not prudent to

WHAT YOUR BROKER NEVER TELLS YOU

implement this strategy in a qualified plan, since these are retirement funds.

The bottom line to this story is that the broker was **"betting the farm"** with *retirement money* - and the client was unaware of the tremendous risk!

The fact is, the traditional relationship between a broker and client carries with it an inherent *"conflict of interest"*. In other words, he is torn between taking care of you and taking care of himself. Consider this for a moment: even though your broker may really care about you and your money, when his mortgage payment is due, whose interest comes first? When push comes to shove, self-preservation—a human reaction—will be the determining factor. A friend of mine in the business was married with three children. After a particularly bad production week, he confided that he had been bemoaning his dismal results to his wife the night before. After hearing her husband's plight, her response was: *"I don't care what you have to do - just don't make less than you did last* **year!"** This incident was not unusual. All of us felt similar pressures. Does this mean that you will get **"bad"** advice? Not necessarily, but whatever investment is recommended to you may serve your broker much better. Since you trust your broker, assuming (sometimes incorrectly) he is more knowledgeable than you, you will usually take his

WHAT YOUR BROKER NEVER TELLS YOU

advice. Here is a more graphic way to visualize what's happening: *See Fig. 2*

I call this the **"self-interest scale"**. It's not hard to see which side gets served first. Let me give you a typical scenario in the business: As a broker, commission income is derived by moving YOUR money around. Let's assume for a moment that I'm back in the business and I'm considering two investments for you. One pays a small commission; the other a large. Which investment do I recommend? It doesn't take a rocket scientist to come up with the answer. Does this mean that the investment that pays me more is necessarily a bad deal for you? Does it mean that I've done anything immoral or unethical? No on both counts. It simply means that you were not given the best and fairest advice because of the conflict between *your goals* and *my pocketbook*. This disparity of interests defines what I term the **"gray area"**. The broker stays "just this side of the line" - nothing immoral or unethical but also not always serving you well, either. A good example might be the difference between recommending a government bond versus a high-quality corporate bond. The government bond pays the broker about twenty-five dollars in gross commissions on a $10,000 trade against almost **four hundred dollars** on the corporate bond trade. Hardly a choice for the broker, is it?! Recognizing this inherent

WHAT YOUR BROKER NEVER TELLS YOU

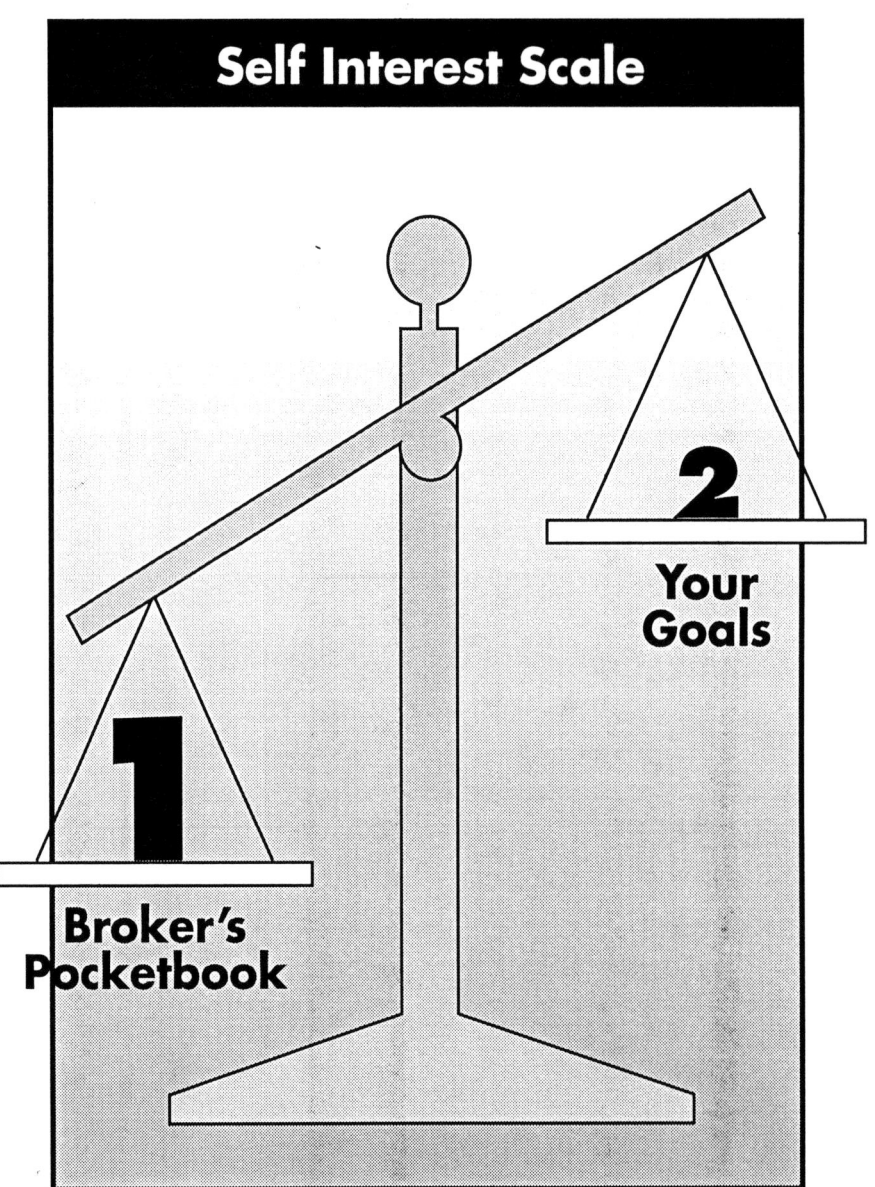

Figure 2

conflict of interest will help you avoid being victimized. The GOOD NEWS is that there are specific ways to avoid this investment trap. Read on to find out how…

RULE #2

Understand that above all else, your broker is a salesperson, not a financial analyst. Your advisor is paid to generate commissions for himself and the firm. Period. He **sells ideas** to you and other clients and is compensated handsomely for his efforts. Almost half the brokers I knew during my tenure in the business had no college degree while a large number had degrees in non-business related areas, such as education. They were hired SIMPLY because they could sell! Investment ideas are merely intangible products that must be moved like any other form of inventory - whether they are Jaguars or farm produce. Here's an example of how unqualified some brokers are: A few of us decided to play a prank on one totally inept person. We huddled next to the coffee machine and, in voices loud enough for him to hear, we spoke excitedly about an impending stock take-over (bogus, of course). We voiced our confidence that the target stock would run up twenty points or more on the announcement, which would be forthcoming at any moment. Predictably, within minutes of our staged conversation, the broker was on the phone with a

WHAT YOUR BROKER NEVER TELLS YOU

client and about to *recommend purchase of the stock*! Luckily, we stopped him in time. I've learned that he is *still* a broker with another firm in a different state. You would be shocked to learn how many stocks are sold on such unsubstantiated rumors. Brokers are just as easily duped by a good story as any investor. **Remember:** brokers are always looking for a story that has a **"hook"**, for example, takeover situations. Why? Because good stories are easily sold on the phone. What is unfortunate, and serves as a gauge of our collective hunger for a quick profit, is that clients want to hear such stories. From the smallest investor to the multimillionaire, the thrill of a "quick hit" is almost irresistible and most certainly intoxicating. We called it the *"JAZZ"*. These stories make listening to a broker offer advice based on sound, fundamental principles seem boring by comparison. Inevitably, these take-over stories are lose-lose situations. Should you actually profit from such a trade, you're probably guilty of insider trading, since acting on information not yet public is considered illegal. And if the information is bad, as it usually is, you're going to lose money anyway. What I found to be true many times over the years is this: When you buy on sound fundamentals principles, you very often stumble on the "big hit" because you just happened to be in the right place at the right time. Buying for the long term will often times give you your best short term gain.

WHAT YOUR BROKER NEVER TELLS YOU

RULE #3

Brokers are under a great deal of pressure, but it's not the kind you're probably thinking of. It isn't the stress of trying to deal with the Bulls and Bears of Wall Street. The REAL pressure is production - how many commission dollars are you bringing in to the firm. So, the **game** for the broker is to generate enough production to:

- Earn fat commissions; and

- Keep the brokerage firm off his back.

Brokers are typically ranked within their firm by quintiles. Each broker is ranked against others with the same length of service. In other words, a first year broker would not be ranked with a twenty year veteran. Here's how it usually breaks down: *See Fig. 3*

To better understand this chart, suppose a firm employs 1,000 brokers. If you were to divide this number by 5, every 200 represents a new quintile, giving you five quintile rankings. For example, if a broker ranked in the top 200, he would be in the 1st quintile. If he ranked in the 500 - 600 range, he would be in the 3rd quintile. Finding yourself in the bottom 200 would be the fifth **(see ya' later)** quintile.

Quintile Rankings

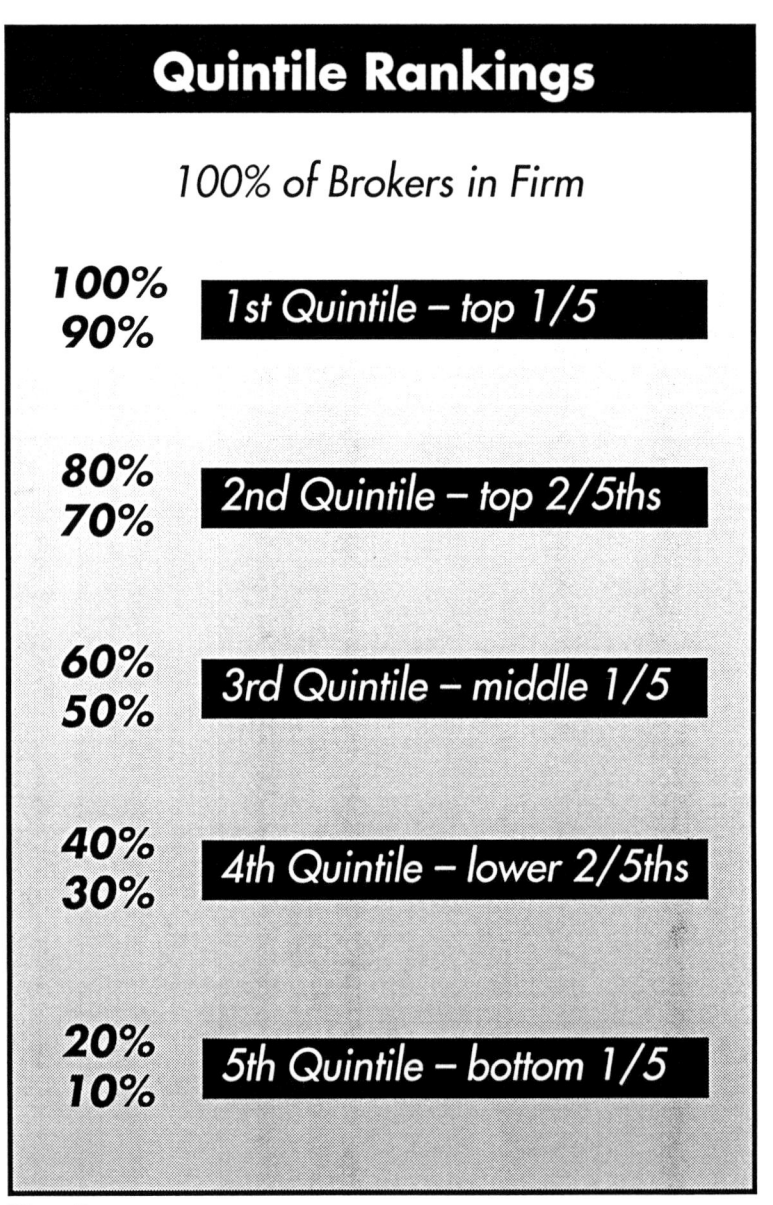

100% of Brokers in Firm

100%
90% — 1st Quintile – top 1/5

80%
70% — 2nd Quintile – top 2/5ths

60%
50% — 3rd Quintile – middle 1/5

40%
30% — 4th Quintile – lower 2/5ths

20%
10% — 5th Quintile – bottom 1/5

Figure 3

WHAT YOUR BROKER NEVER TELLS YOU

Such ranking breeds conflict of interest. Here's why:

- If your broker's in the **first or second quintile**, he's on safe ground because he's generating a mountain of revenue for the firm.

- If he's in the **third quintile**, the manager and/or sales manager are now acting a little less friendly, but he's still OK for now.

- By the **fourth quintile**, it's being suggested (not too subtly) that falling any lower in the rankings is not advisable - bad for his **"financial health"**, so to speak.

- By **fifth quintile**, it's desperation time. No more slaps on the back, "How ya doin'?" from management. The word comes down: You now have one quarter (three months) to get back into the fourth quintile or your history.

If he can't turn it around in 90 days - and most brokers can't - simply clean out your desk and call a taxi. Many brokers are routinely let go at fifth quintile without any grace period or chance for redemption,. Make no mistake: the brokerage business is **not** a charitable enterprise. Genuine concern for your clients because the market happened in a free-fall and you did not want to expose them to any unnecessary risks won't cut it. Your legitimate concern for your clients is irrelevant. You must simply do business, period! Every firm knows exactly what it takes to **"fill a desk"**. In other words, it is very much aware of the revenue it needs to break even on every broker.

The broker, qualified or not, is merely the gateway to profit. If he doesn't measure up to the demands placed on him, the exit is to the left of the water cooler. There are brokerage houses that don't use the quintile system anymore. They've quantified a different set of guidelines, for example, based on percentage of goals set. The bottom line is that they're still ranked.

Is this **conflict of interest** phenomenon becoming clear to you? For the relatively new brokers that haven't been around very long, this places a tremendous amount of pressure on them to do business. They have a limited number of clients and can call them only so often with recommendations. So when they are pressed to do more business to keep their jobs, they start making mistakes and talking their clients into bad decisions because THEY need the production (commissions). Then they talk themselves into believing that what they did was OK - when deep down they know better. I've been there, I know.

WHAT YOUR BROKER NEVER TELLS YOU

You might assume that a broker that has been around a long time is under less pressure because he has more clients and a larger pool of money to tap into. To a degree you would be right. At the same time, however, every broker - new and old - starts out on January 1st with a big **"zero"** on the commission run and a pay-out (described in Chapter 2) that goes back down to the lowest level. Neither the rookie nor the veteran wants to produce and make less than the previous year. In fact, over the ten years I spent in the business, production never, NEVER came easy, and I was always in the first or second quintile. I was friends with several of the "older" brokers who were in the business fifteen years or more and I kept assuming that the pressure on them would lessen. Not so. The reality was that they scrambled for business just as much as I did. To gauge the truth of this, make a mental note of the time of the month when your broker tends to contact you. If you find that calls are coming near the month's end, you can bet the farm that he needs more commissions to meet the demands of his firm and/or his pocketbook.

The reasons for wanting to achieve big numbers every year varies from individual to individual. Some of the reasons are financial, such as maintaining a certain life style. Some are ego driven, such as holding a certain rank within the office or the firm. Or maybe winning the trips that accompany reaching certain production levels turns the broker on. It did for me. Going on first-class vacations and rubbing elbows with the best in the business was a real high.

Lastly, please understand that intelligence is not a measuring stick of success as a broker. Some of the people in the industry that I knew had trouble igniting two brain cells and yet they were in the first quintile, earning $300,000 - $400,000 per year. At the same time, some of the brightest people in the business were fired because they couldn't produce commissions fast enough. I truly believe that many of the people I saw let go were many times more intelligent than I was, both in terms of general knowledge and financial acumen.

POINTS TO REMEMBER:

- Be certain that you use a broker that has been around awhile - at least ten years. Longevity means that he has been through several market cycles - both up and down. Newer brokers that have only experienced bull markets think that anything that they recommend will go up! This aspect is critical to your long-term success in the market. Seasoned brokers that have been through brutally bearish markets have a much better sense of timing and a keen understanding of what down markets can do to their clients and ultimately to themselves. Let the younger brokers make their mistakes on someone else!

To give you an idea of just how hungry I was as a new broker, a gentleman came in off the street and wanted to open an account, which thrilled me! He proceeded to sit down at my desk, reached under his pant leg and pulled **$500 in cash out of his sock**. I'll never forget it because it was a hot day and the cash was all sweaty! Being new and eager for any type of account, I gladly accepted it. A few years later, even considering this type of situation would be out of the question.

- *Remember!* A broker is a salesperson, not an analyst. Too many of us confuse the roles. Take his advice at face value and double check it with outside sources as well as your own gut instincts. Most of the time, all he'll be doing is regurgitating what the in-house analysts have said. We'll talk more about this in Chapter Four.

- Discuss - **in depth** - what you hope to accomplish. Sound self-evident? You would be amazed at the number of people with scant idea of why they are investing. If asked, they usually respond with this mundane truism: **"I want to make money"**. An annual return of 15% - 20% is a

WHAT YOUR BROKER NEVER TELLS YOU

typical, hoped for objective. Yet, when pressed further, they will concede that stocks leave them confused and fearful. Asked whether they could tolerate a loss — the response is near-apoplexy. Ironically, if you are an investor, you already know that high returns are not likely if you are risk-aversive. Sorry, but you simply can't have it both ways. Greater returns carry with it greater risks. If the parties involved are not clear about the objectives, disappointment - and a complaint invariably follows. Be certain that you reconcile in your heart and mind what you hope to gain against the amount of risk you want to assume. This is YOUR responsibility!

- It is a **MUST** that you are comfortable with your investment choices. If stocks and bonds are within your comfort zone, be wary if you are approached with something esoteric, such as options-trading or a private placement railroad car sale/lease-back tax shelter offering the "potential" for exceptionally high write-offs. These investments can be made to sound quite attractive, but they also diminish the importance of a tried and true approach. **Rule #405** of the securities code is **"Know Your Customer"** and it means that your broker is obligated to know as much about you, your temperament, and your financial situation as he can so that he can make

WHAT YOUR BROKER NEVER TELLS YOU

SUITABLE recommendations based upon the information you have furnished him. If he suggests anything that seems out of line with the parameters you have given him, a red flag should go up. **Groth Law #1**: If you don't understand how the market works or have the slightest discomfort with it - stay away! Or better yet, take a vacation and spend the money you planned to invest on yourself. Your "gut feeling" is usually right on target.

- Keep close track of:

  A) your net profit and losses for the year; and

  B) total commissions paid for the year.

Suppose your $100,000 portfolio grows **20%** net in one year, and the commissions paid amount to $8,000. So what?! If you can net this high return every year, you're very lucky. It's when your gain is only $3,000 **(3%)** and you shelled out the same $8,000 that it's time to reexamine your position.

Always check your monthly statement to be sure that the positions listed are the ones you authorized for purchase or sale. Be aware that there are two types of accounts, **discretionary** and **non-discretionary**. Discretionary accounts require you to fill out papers giving permission for the broker to buy and sell as he sees fit, based on the parameters you set,

WHAT YOUR BROKER NEVER TELLS YOU

without talking with you first. Non-discretionary accounts mean that you must give your explicit consent for any purchase or sales, either in person or over the phone. These accounts are the most prevalent.

Unthinkable... but *true*:

This story is so incredible that you may have trouble believing it...

A million dollar producer I knew personally would routinely buy large investments, usually unit investment trusts, in the **NON-DISCRETIONARY** accounts of his wealthy clients. So what's wrong with that? HE NEVER INFORMED THEM OF THE TRADE OR OBTAINED THEIR CONSENT!!! He simply made the trade in the account and hoped the client wouldn't notice! This particular investment was chosen because it was a big ticket (commission) item and a relatively stable security that paid monthly interest checks to the account. The trade I witnessed totaled more than $100,000! Now, if you're still receiving oxygen into your brain you must be asking yourself: "How could someone not notice that a $100,000 *underline*unauthorized trade*underline* had been made in their account?" Some clients DID notice, and when they called him to inquire about the irregularity, this slick broker nonchalantly said that it must have been an "account number error" and purchased in their account "by mistake". But wait, it gets better!...

He would then send through the wire operator an account number change and "move" the investment into another unsuspecting client's account! If this customer called regarding the unauthorized trade, they simply were told the same story and the investment was "moved" again... and again... until some thoughtless client forgot to check his statement. This point is **CRITICAL** to remember: Since he traded $100,000 in cash for $100,000 of an investment, the total VALUE of the account at month end didn't substantially change, did it? Look at it this way: *See Fig. 4*

If the client is ONLY looking at the bottom line value of his account, he may not notice any change in the totals of the portfolio mix. You may ask: "What about the trade confirmation statement that would have gone out to the customer **CONFIRMING** the trade?" Excellent question. The unfortunate reality is that active investors are inundated with reams of mail everyday from the brokerage house. I know from experience that many of my clients **NEVER** opened their mail. They would simply bring it in to me and ask me what this or that was. In talking with other brokers, they too were shocked at how little attention the average client paid to his account. Can you imagine the door of opportunity this opens

Sample Account

BEFORE TRADE	AFTER TRADE
$500,000	VS. $400,000

Money Market (cash)

$200,000	VS. $300,000

Securities

$700,000	VS. $700,000

TOTAL

Figure 4

WHAT YOUR BROKER NEVER TELLS YOU

for a dishonest broker? The broker mentioned above KNEW which clients of his were naive and trusting, so this scam was (and still is) easy to pull-off. If that doesn't scare you, he's still out there ringing-up **$2,500,000 *PER YEAR*** in gross commissions......

Sound bizarre? It happens every day. A very high percentage of investors *never* look at their monthly statements! And the ones that do either don't look close enough or don't understand what they are looking at. Incidentally, don't think that the story mentioned above only happens to those clients with large accounts — I saw it happen with accounts much smaller than the one illustrated. No one is beyond the reach of the greedy...

Be aware that all commissions will not show up on your confirmation statement because they are "included" in the net price of the investment. That is why they are called "net trades". Before we focus on how to determine the commission you pay for every investment, here's another story that demonstrates the perfidy of many brokers in the industry...

I will **never** forget this experience because it left such a mark on my awareness of the business. In retrospect, I believe it ultimately caused me to leave the industry. As a green and naive broker I had occasion to talk with a seasoned broker who befriended me. One day at lunch, I asked him how to go about making my very few clients tons of money, thinking that this would be the best way to endear them to me. His response floored me.

> **"Dick", he said, "the best case scenario is to hope your clients stay even. If they make too much, they'll take the money and run. If they lose too much, they'll go to someone else."**

I was stunned. This simply made no sense to me, a rookie broker with stars in his eyes. But when you consider the "recommendations" brokers receive from their analysts (more on this in Chapter Four) and pass on to their clients, this scenario pretty much takes care of itself! Not coincidentally, ten years later, as I reviewed my biggest accounts, most were indeed close to even. The game of poker is a fitting analogy. Take a minute and think about the poker players you know, one's who may have played with the same group of people for five, ten, or even twenty years. After most games, if you asked any one of them how he did, he would probably tell you that he **"broke even"**. Huge wins or losses will cause most players to drop out, but as long as

WHAT YOUR BROKER NEVER TELLS YOU

you stay close to even, you can play forever. So it goes with investors. They want to keep playing the game, focusing less on multiplying their chips and more on "not losing". Moderate gains whet your appetite while moderate losses compel you to try and get your money back. Interesting, yet perplexing, is the fact that most investors don't follow investment results very closely, especially over a long period of time. They tend to selectively remember the winners and forget the losers. Many top producers I knew said that they, too, were aware of this phenomenon. Clients will stay loyal to their brokers for any number of reasons, **none** of which have anything to do with investment performance. Their broker may by nice to them, listening to their problems whenever they call, answering questions, and generally being a **friend**. This is an admirable trait for a broker to have. Just don't forget how the game is being played. This could be an **expensive** friendship.

The bottom line is simply this: if you're going to play the investment game… **play to win** - consistently - year after year. Before we look at ways to make that happen, let's examine a few more obstacles that will stand in your way.

CHAPTER TWO
THE BROKERAGE HOUSE

> *Who's Money Is It Anyway?...*

CHAPTER TWO

As we've noted earlier in the text, brokers are salespeople, not analysts. The question arises: What kind of person does the brokerage house look for when trying to **"fill a desk"**? Your assumption is correct: obviously someone who knows how to deliver a slick and compelling sales pitch. Former and current life insurance sales representatives are heavily recruited. I know this to be true from experience, since I sold insurance very successfully before becoming a stock broker. I had innate selling skills which served me well. Be assured, though, that my success as a broker did not rest on any broad knowledge of the investment business. I personified the expression **"fake it til ya' make it"**. I literally *sold* my way to success, as do most brokers.

Every newly-hired broker faces the daunting Series 7 Exam, a strenuous, six-hour ordeal which requires many months of preparation. After passing the exam, he must meet certain requirements established by the brokerage house within a specified time frame or he will be let go. These requirements are wholly profit-oriented, combining a variety of factors, such as commissions generated to the firm, assets under management, number of new accounts, etc. Ultimately, however, commissions are the bottom line. Produce and you stay; do otherwise and you're gone. Period. New brokers came and went at such a frantic pace that my friends and I

WHAT YOUR BROKER NEVER TELLS YOU

Revolving Door

WHAT YOUR BROKER NEVER TELLS YOU

laughed at this **"revolving door"** process, sad as it was.

Older brokers advised us not to bother learning the names of the new brokers until they survived the first year. Callous? You bet! But this business is not for thin-skinned, unpragmatic people. Often, during my first year I, too, fretted about survival, and I believe that this fear impelled me to become a top producer. The irony is that no broker can instantly gain the trust of a new client. It takes time, like any other relationship. And yet, the brokerage firm expects instant results. A case in point: My biggest client initially opened a money-market fund which pays no commission. *Two years* passed before he acted on any of my recommendations for which I was paid. Amazingly, he became a $30,000 per-year account. At my pay-out level, I netted a tidy $12,000 in yearly income- and that was only one account out of hundreds!

Today, more and more of the full service brokerage houses are **"suggesting"** that their brokers push **"proprietary products"** to their clients. These are usually investment products designed and brought to the market by the brokerage house. For example, one of its' own mutual funds, real estate limited partnerships, tax shelters, etc. Because it is an **"in house"** product, all the money stays within the firm, and the broker usually receives a higher pay-out on these

WHAT YOUR BROKER NEVER TELLS YOU

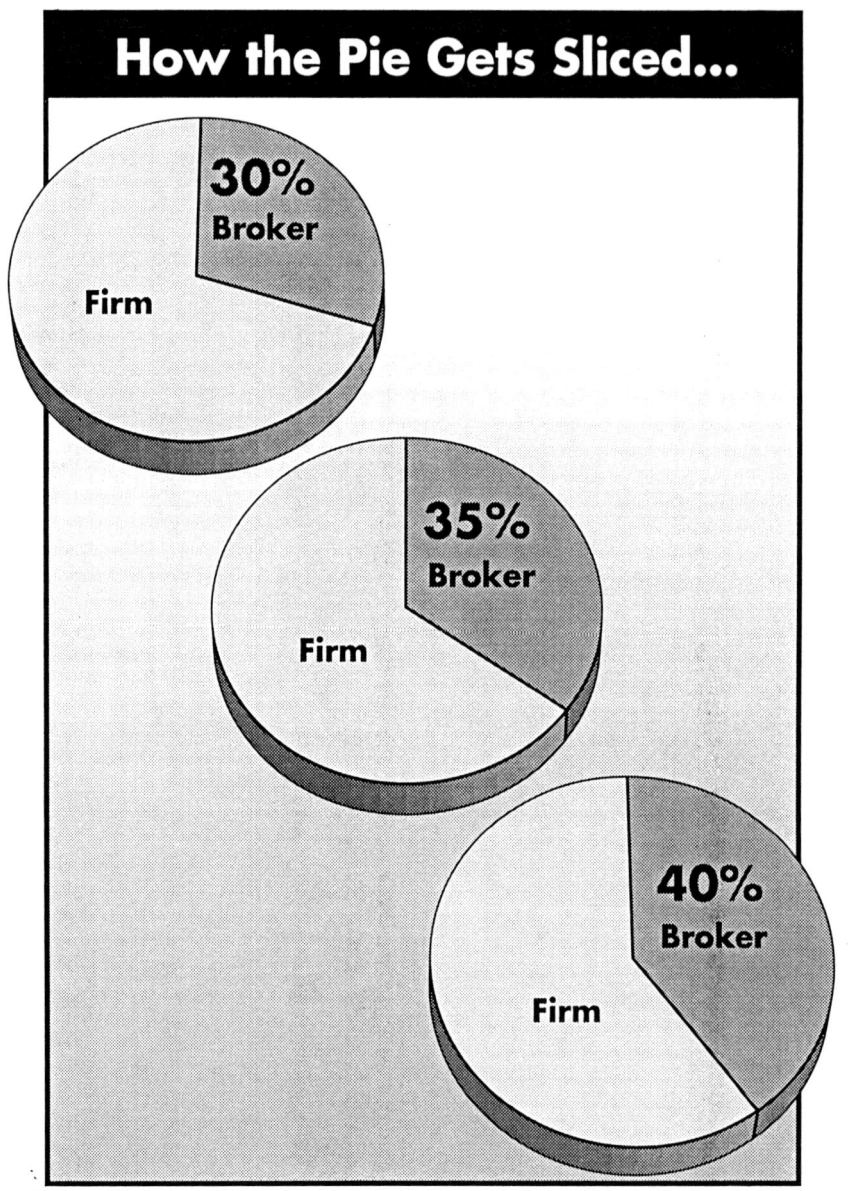

How the Pie Gets Sliced...

30% Broker / Firm

35% Broker / Firm

40% Broker / Firm

Figure 5

WHAT YOUR BROKER NEVER TELLS YOU

products. Compare this to a broker who sells an **"outside"** mutual fund, like Templeton, for example. Part of the sales charge (commission) must go to Templeton as its' fee, so consequently, the brokerage house receives less and so does the broker. In short, the pie has to be split more ways. The brokerage house **"discourages"** this practice by restructuring the broker's commission grid. This means that the broker can sell any product he wishes, but he'll **make less money** (smaller pay-out) on those products not in house.

Think about the position this puts **you** in as the investor. You're trusting your broker to give you solid, **unbiased** investment advice. But because of the manner in which he's paid, you will probably wind up getting advice to buy investment products that will better compensate **him**. Doesn't seem fair, does it? Once again, that pesky **conflict of interest** rears its ugly head. There **IS** a way around this, so don't give up yet! Read on…

HOW THE PIE GETS SLICED…

Commissions generated to the firm are formulated on a split arrangement. *See Fig. 5*

While company policies vary, most firms start their brokers on January 1st earning roughly thirty percent commission for

WHAT YOUR BROKER NEVER TELLS YOU

every dollar brought in. As the year progresses and the production (commission) increases, so does the pay-out to the broker. It's possible to achieve a fifty per cent pay out (even higher at certain firms) if the production is high enough. The top producer at my first firm generated gross revenues in the area of **$15,000,000** in one year, netting him more than **$7,500,00** in personal income! Obviously, he reigned as one of the top guns in the entire industry. Such personal income is certainly not the norm.

A relatively new broker producing $150,000 in annual gross commissions would end the year with approximately a 35% pay-out, meaning he would earn about $52,000. A seasoned producer generating $500,000 in gross commissions would earn well above $200,000. It should be abundantly clear by now that commissions are the key to survival. Here is a scenario that demonstrates the point:

> Assume your broker phoned six months ago and recommended purchasing 1,000 shares of XYZ stock at $25. Today, the stock is worth $30, and you're $5,000 richer, less commissions, of course. Now your broker phones to suggest that you **sell** XYZ and **buy** ABC, whose prospects **"look good"**! (?) Since you've made about 20% in six months, should you sell and reinvest the money into the new stock?

WHAT YOUR BROKER NEVER TELLS YOU

Perhaps. Perhaps not. The real question is *why* should you make this change? More importantly, why is your broker suggesting a **change in strategy**? Heaven forbid, could it possibly be to earn a "round trip" trade - two quick commissions, one on the buy and one on the sell? I have to be honest - I loved "round trip" trades. This was easy money, and I justified my recommendations with the rationale **"you never go broke taking a profit".** While this is obviously true, most of the time the stock that was sold went significantly higher over the long-term. Here is where we enter that **"gray area"** spoken of previously. The broker is always pressing for commissions. The hunger for another trade precludes patience. The broker can't wait another year or so for the XYZ stock to go higher, he needs the commission *NOW!* Ironically, time is a broker's best asset; yet, the conditions within the brokerage house work against it.

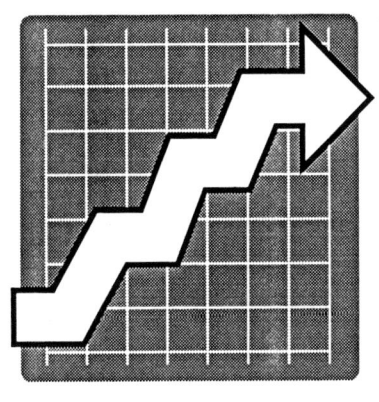

Even though you may have doubts about changing stocks, rest assured your broker has convinced himself that NOW is the right time. In all fairness, your broker may be entirely correct in making a sell recommendation. But before you agree to any transaction, key questions must be asked...

- Has the stock reached the target price you envisioned when you originally bought it? If you're in a strong bull market, your stock may get carried along with the tide.

- Is there a specific reason to believe that the stock might fall, such as talk of bad earnings, or the firm's analysts going to a "sell" recommendation which would drive the stock price lower?

- Where's resistance on the stock? Is it there yet? *See Fig. 6*

- Could you cover your position by selling a call option against the stock?

- If the stock pays a dividend, when is the next ex-date?

- What is the **current opinion** from your brokerage house?

- Why not place a stop-loss order to protect the downside?

These are just a few questions that must be **asked** and **answered** if you expect to *"win"* this game. Experience taught me that, most of the time, investors sell too soon, and the stock they replace it with is a "dog with fleas" - à la Gordon Gecco in "Wall Street". Always remember this axiom:

Support VS. Resistance

Resistance

Best Time To Sell

Stock Price: 25, 20, 15, 10, 5, 0

Best Time To Buy

Support

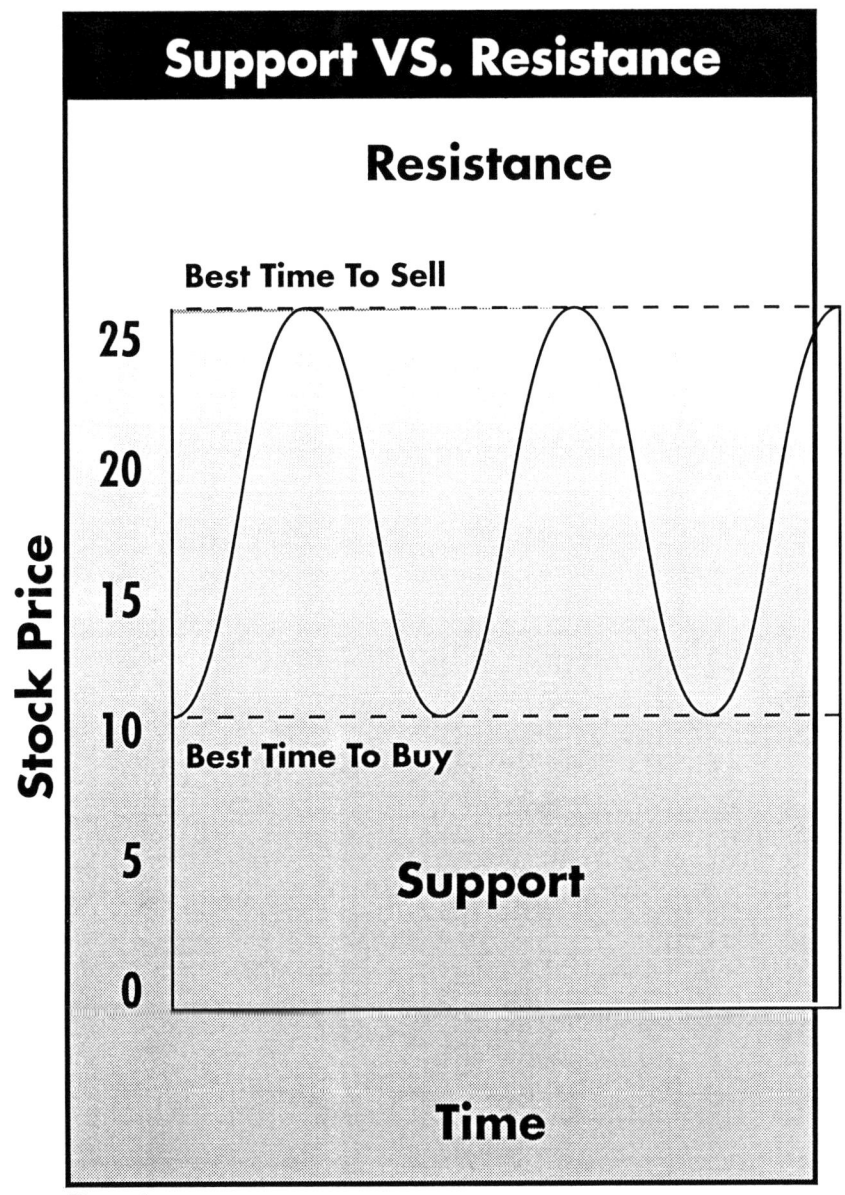

Time

Figure 6

WHAT YOUR BROKER NEVER TELLS YOU

"Cut your losses short and let your profits ride." Recognize that sell/buy decisions are two separate transactions. If you are comfortable with owning ABC stock, buy it. If you have to sell the old stock in order to finance the new purchase, red flags should go up. Be aware that brokers - ever the salesman - will present it as a package deal. Ask yourself this question:

- "What are the odds that XYZ has reached its perfect price and time to sell **AND** ABC is now at the perfect price and time to buy???"

Hello, is anybody home?! *Nothing* is ever that perfect.

It bears reminding that the ethics and morality of your broker and his firm are irrelevant. They're playing their game and you MUST play yours. Reality is the essence of the game. Translation: **YOUR MONEY IS ALWAYS UP FOR GRABS.**

BROKERAGE HOUSES: A Difference

There are two types of brokerage houses: Full service operations, "Rhinos" such as Merrill Lynch, Dean Witter, Payne Webber, and discounters, like Schwab, Olde, etc. Full service brokerage firms offer, among other services, their own

WHAT YOUR BROKER NEVER TELLS YOU

research department, along with a broker to lead you to the promised land. For all this "service" you will pay heavy commissions. Discounters, on the other hand, execute the trade and that's the end of it. Since you're not paying for advice, the commissions charged are much less. If you're informed enough to make your own investment decisions, it's probably best and certainly less costly to use a discounter. However, if you must rely on the expanded services of the bigger houses, don't be shy about asking for a discount. Be mindful, however, that if you only make a few trades a year, it may be difficult to get one. But, if you're a regular player and generate more than one thousand dollars a year in commissions, you should receive anywhere from a five to thirty per cent discount on exchange transactions, i.e. stocks, listed bonds, options, etc. The amount of the discount is **always** negotiable. Ask your broker about his discount policy. If he hedges and claims he doesn't have one, press him for a full answer. Don't be swayed by evasion. Brokers disdain discounts since it means less money in their pockets. Most investors are unaware of discount advantages, naively assuming that their account is too insignificant, and thus are too embarrassed to ask. Amazingly enough during my career, many of my clients (even multimillionaires) believed that their accounts were among the smallest and that I managed much more affluent people.

WHAT YOUR BROKER NEVER TELLS YOU

If you expect to *win* the game, it's vital to understand how commissions are handled.

Now, let's find out how you can keep on top of your account...

CHAPTER THREE

INVESTMENT PRODUCTS

A Great Place For Commissions To Hide...

CHAPTER THREE

The following is a breakdown of the various investment products most prevalent within the industry and their respective commission costs. We will be concentrating on those investments that show no evidence of a commission on the transaction statement. Knowing how these charges affect the bottom line are key to your success...

- **LISTED TRANSACTIONS:** These investments are traded on an exchange, such as the New York Stock Exchange, the Midwest, Pacific, CBOE, etc. Being on an exchange means that it operates under an auction system, with buyers and sellers screaming out how much they will be willing to buy or sell for. This system assures the investor the best chance of obtaining a fair price. Transactions such as stocks, options, commodities, and listed bonds will show the commission on the transaction (or confirmation) statement. These are very easy to keep track of. The difficulty arises when other investment products are purchased, such as non-listed bonds, mutual funds, closed-end unit trusts, annuities, new stock issues, and tax shelters. All of them have charges, or commissions, **"built"** into the product and are termed "net trades". Each of the above mentioned securities, with the exception of non-listed bonds, are required by law to provide the investor with a prospectus prior to the purchase. This document discloses all of the charges. Yet, most people never read it, filled as it is with jargon and obscure investment terms. If you have ever looked at a prospectus, you'll understand what a daunting challenge it is to grasp its meaning.

- **UNIT INVESTMENT TRUSTS:** This product will usually compensate the broker $2\frac{1}{2}$ to $3\frac{1}{2}$ points per unit. Translated, this means that he receives production credit (gross commissions) of $25 - $35 per unit. This charge has some leeway that is arbitrarily set by the brokerage house. For example, if a unit sells for $1,092 and you purchase ten units, it will cost you $10,920, plus accrued interest (this part will be explained later). No commission is evidenced, since this is a "net" trade, but the broker still earns $250 - $350. As mentioned earlier, a "net" trade means that the commission is included in the cost of the transaction, so you're completely in the dark about how much your broker earned on the transaction. How convenient! In this example, if the broker took the maximum (I always did) and he was in the 35% pay-out range, then he'd earn $122.50 (35% of $350) for what was probably a two minute phone call. Is it possible to determine how much the charge was? Certainly. Simply look in the prospectus that **you** should have requested **BEFORE** you

WHAT YOUR BROKER NEVER TELLS YOU

made the purchase. This is one of those situations in which you need to know what to ask for in advance. We'll talk more about this particular product later in the book.

- **MUTUAL FUNDS:** Charges on this investment will range from one half per cent to eight per cent. The broker will also be given a higher pay-out - a bigger piece of the pie - if he sells in-house funds (proprietary products) which are offered and managed by the brokerage house itself. As discussed in the previous chapter, since the firm doesn't have to split any of the fees with an outside, independent portfolio manager, it can better reward the broker. Conversely, outside funds are managed by an independent portfolio manager not associated with the brokerage house. Examples of this type of fund would include familiar names, such as Templeton, Dreyfuss, Putnam, Van Guard, etc.

Mutual funds are classified as **load** and **no-load**. Loaded funds offer two choices: Front-end or back-end loads. Front-end charges take the commissions off the top of the money you initially invest and that's it. The more money you invest, the lower the sales charge will be. These are known as **"break points"**. Back-end charges assess no fees going in, but charge you a fee if you take your money out within a certain time frame. For example, you might be charged seven percent if you take out your money in the first year, six percent in year two, five percent in year three, etc. After the seventh year, there is no charge upon selling. The broker still gets his money up front, but the commission is amortized over time through the internal charges of the fund. Be very wary of any broker that wants you to sell your mutual fund and place the proceeds in another investment - especially **another** mutual fund. You would be amazed at the number of people that agree to sell their fund and have no idea how much it's costing them in fees. Check yourself by asking these questions:

- Will there be a **surrender charge** upon selling? If so, how much?

- Will there be a **capitol gain or loss**?

- **Why** am I being asked to sell?

- What is being suggested as a replacement for these funds? **Why???**

- Have my **objectives changed**?

- Has there been a **change in my financial situation**?

- Is the fund no longer **performing** up to my expectations?

WHAT YOUR BROKER NEVER TELLS YOU

After answering these questions, there **may** be a legitimate reason to sell the fund and do something else with the money. Usually, if you are the one questioning the investment, the reasons for making a change tend to be more compelling. If the broker is making a case for change, all the red flags should go up and it's time to do your homework!

Question: is there such a thing as no-load funds? Technically, yes, but do you really believe a portfolio manager would handle your money without charging a fee? If you read your prospectus you will discover a small item known as 12B1 charges. These fees are charged against the performance of the fund to pay the manager's fee, expenses, etc. This expense (and you thought this was a no-load!) can vary widely among all the funds available to you. Obviously, then, a no-load simply means that there are no front-end charges. Your goal should be to find a well run fund with a low expense charge. However, don't assume that low charges and good performance are one and the same. Some of the funds that I recommended to my clients were among the highest front-end loads, yet they were stellar performers as well. Sometimes, you get what you pay for. In the end, try to strike a balance between a fund with good, consistent performance and one that isn't too expense-heavy.

- **ANNUITIES:** Most annuities sold today have rear-end

surrender charges, meaning that there is no charge going in, but if you surrender the contract before a certain time, you will incur a declining charge similar to those in a mutual fund. The broker still gets his money up front, just as he does in a mutual fund. Someone has to pay the freight. Guess who? That's why it is important to look at the **internal charges** of the contract. A few still have front-end charges varying from 2% to 5% (or more) of the money invested. Annuities can be either fixed or variable. Fixed annuities place your money in the general account of the insurance company that is issuing it. As long as the insurance company is strong financially, this is considered very safe. A variable annuity maintains the same tax-deferred status as the fixed, except your money is placed in a mutual fund for potentially higher growth. As with any mutual fund, there is market risk. It is **crucial** that you examine the internal charges before committing any money. These charges can be brutally high. Be especially wary of any annuity that offers an **exceptionally high rate** of return compared to other annuities in the marketplace. These annuities are most likely replete with "junk bonds" - risky securities, to be sure. For those unfamiliar with junk bond, these are the very same securities that put many S & L's in serious jeopardy. These bonds are issued by companies that are in financial trouble. In order to get financing and raise money in the marketplace, they have to offer an above average return. This is OK - **as long as they stay in business!**

- **NON-LISTED BONDS:** Whether corporates or municipals, these investments are the hardest to track. Let's compare these with a listed bond - one that trades on the New York Bond Exchange. Here you will pay the normal exchange rates (commissions) and the charge will show up on your confirmation statement after the trade. You can check the paper every day to see the bid and ask price for the bond, as is the case with stocks. No problem so far...

It's the unlisted bonds that pose a quandary for the investor and a gold mine for the broker. Most investors are unaware that there are more unlisted bonds than listed. These non-listed bonds are held in the inventory of the member firm. This means that after a public offering of a bond, rather than have it listed on the NYSE bond exchange, member firms will hold bonds in their inventory (for purchase and sale) and **"make a market"** for the security. Since there is no daily public auction (as on the exchange) to establish a price, the only way to check its price is to call your broker and have him call the bond trader at his firm. Now the logical question is:

WHAT YOUR BROKER NEVER TELLS YOU

- "**How am I going to inquire about a bond that I don't even know exists?**" The answer is: **you won't**.

Most people own non-listed bonds because their broker called and **suggested they buy them**. Ironically, there could be two bonds issued by the same corporation, with one listed and the other not. Odds are that you will be discussing the non-listed bond because - unknown to you - the mark-up is much greater. Here's an example:

Your broker scans the bond inventory sheet that is circulated every day and notes that the XYZ 6's of 2010 are bid at par with a point. Translated, this means that the bond sells for $1,000 (known as "par") and the broker stands to earn $10 commission on each bond sold. Sounds fair and reasonable so far, right? But here's the rub: Unknown to you, the broker can tell the trader he wants four points on the deal. The bond price now rises to $1,030 — an **EXTRA 3%**— and the broker now receives $40 per bond gross commission. Since most trades involve at least ten bonds, you're now paying an **EXTRA $300** more for the bonds and generously putting the overblown profit on your brokers production run. Consider this: the commission for the same LISTED bond offered on the exchange would be closer to $100 for ten bonds. Why wouldn't you know this? Simple: Since the broker was kind enough to include the commission in the price of the bond, your confirmation statement will show **"0"**

WHAT YOUR BROKER NEVER TELLS YOU

under the heading "commission/mark-up". How magnanimous, don't you agree? As explained in the unit trust section, this is also known as a "net" trade. Commissions never show up. In addition, there will usually be an extra ¼ or ½ point commission on the sell side ($25 to $50 per ten bonds). Again, none of these amounts will show up either because they are net trades as well. As an investor, if the confirmation shows no commission, you would tend to think that there were none. Not so.

ABSURD EXCESSES PRODUCE OPPORTUNITIES...

In the 1980's, I made a great deal of money selling bonds. You may find it interesting to know that virtually *none* of my clients were bond buyers when we first became acquainted. I introduced them to bonds by bringing this investment alternative to the table. Interest rates in the 80's were 16% - 18% and I firmly believed that they had to come down because interest costs were hurting almost every business. Try to recall your Econ 101 class. Remember the inverse relationship between interest rates and bond prices? As rates rise, bond prices fall and conversely when interest rates fall, bond prices subsequently rise. Bearing this in mind, I heavily weighted my clients portfolios with bonds using the rationale that if interest rates remained constant, how wrong could I be locking them into investments paying 16% or more? If rates had gone

WHAT YOUR BROKER NEVER TELLS YOU

any higher, the backs of many businesses would have been broken. I believed that it was a low risk proposition. As with most situations that reach extremes, interest rates DID fall... and quite dramatically. (I SUSPECTED that rates were about to crash when I tried to encourage my clients to buy **INSURED CD's** at **17%** and they chortled and said that they wanted to wait because they believed interest rates were going *HIGHER*!)

When everyone is running in the same direction, go the other way! FAST!

Given this falling interest rate scenario, the bondholders in my example profited significantly in two ways:

- They earned 16% or more interest on their money, **PRO-RATED DAILY**, and

- They earned a capital gain when they sold the bond at a profit.

It's important that you understand how bond interest is paid and why bonds can be such an attractive investment under certain conditions:

Assume that the bond coupon, or stated rate of interest, is 10% and you bought ten bonds at par, or $1,000 each. You

WHAT YOUR BROKER NEVER TELLS YOU

would then receive $1,000 per year in interest, $500 every six months. This is considered interest income. Let's also assume that you received your last check on June 1st, and the next check is due December 1st. If you were to sell your bonds on November 30th, does that mean that you forfeit 182 days of accrued interest? The answer is no. Upon the sale of the bond, all the interest earned since the last payment, appropriately called **ACCRUED INTEREST**, would be included in the proceeds of the sale. Consider the ramifications: if the bond were sold for a profit, you would realize a capital gain on your investment as well as interest on your money while you waited! Compare this with a stock sale. If the stock were sold one day before the ex-date, the stockholder would lose the entire quarterly dividend. Obviously, given the right circumstances, bonds can hold a tremendous advantage over stocks. I literally had clients earning 40% - 50% on their money within a six to nine month period! Here was a unique situation and truly a win-win proposition, one that happens very seldom. I had no problem marking up bonds three or four points and earning a great deal of money - I felt justified because my clients shared the good fortune. Since I was paid handsomely for my expertise, did I do a bad job for them? I don't think so. And yet an informed client could have bought these same bonds for **3% - 4% less,** *with no risk*, since it was pure cost! Read on...

WHAT YOUR BROKER NEVER TELLS YOU

Anyone's portfolio could use this extra yield. In other words, it's easier to **lower your transaction costs** by three to four percent than it is to **raise the yield and/or capital gain** by the same amount, because one is controllable (transaction costs) and one isn't (the markets). Look at it this way: if you were to walk into a new car showroom and find the car of your dreams - color, style, options, etc. - and write out a check for the sticker price, would you be buying a **"bad"** car? Not likely. Would you be paying too much for it? Probably. The truism still applies: your money is always up for grabs. Had you understood the rules of the game, you would have known that - in most cases - the sticker price is inflated and can be negotiated down. The same is true for unlisted bonds. **The question is:** how do you know what constitutes a fair price for these bonds?

YOU ALWAYS HAVE TO SHOP AROUND...

Here's some informed advice: the next time your broker calls with a bond idea (either corporate or municipal), write down the complete name of the bond, the coupon, maturity date, and price he quoted you. Tell him you'll consider it. Next, call several brokerage houses and obtain prices on this same bond, letting each know that you are obtaining competitive bids. Don't reveal any prices you've received. In an effort to

WHAT YOUR BROKER NEVER TELLS YOU

entice you to trade with him, another broker may offer a great price. Two variables will affect the price of the bond: the number of bonds the trader has in inventory and to what extent are bonds are marked-up. **Remember:** Bond traders are paid on their performance, just like brokers. The bond department must be profitable just like any other department in the firm. On any given day, the trader may be willing to give you a better price. After getting competitive bids, also check the bond in question against a similar bond listed in the New York Bond Exchange section of the Wall Street Journal or Barrons. Make sure that you compare the following:

- Bonds with the same rating

- Identical coupons

- Identical maturity dates

Unless there is a hidden call date coming up, you will have another good benchmark price with which to compare. Here is where your homework will pay off. After making the phone calls and checking the paper, you will have a solid idea of what a fair price is. Don't be surprised if the best price you've gotten is now $20 to $50 per bond lower than the original quote. If your broker's price was the lowest, congratulations. He's an honest person. Chances are, however, he's not all that innocent. In that case, simply say that you found a better

WHAT YOUR BROKER NEVER TELLS YOU

price on the bond at another firm (terrifying news to most brokers!) and that if he can match it, the trade is his. If he can't or refuses, simply buy the bond from the other broker and tell him to register and ship the bond to you. In this manner, when you receive it, you can deposit it with your current broker and avoid having two separate accounts.

By shopping around, you should be able to save about **$30 per bond.** On the surface, this lower cost may seem insignificant, but consider: an extra $30 commission on a $1,000 bond is 3%, but on a bond selling at $800, the same $30 represents $3\frac{3}{4}$ % This average of $3\frac{1}{2}$ % could mean the difference between a 10% year-end return or a $13\frac{1}{2}$ % return. The difference is considerable. To a professional money manager, the added return is analogous to hitting a grand slam versus a single. But the ramifications go even further…

Let's take a look at **two** purchases of the **same bond** with a $7\frac{1}{2}$ % coupon, one is bought at $102\frac{1}{4}$ and the other at $105\frac{1}{4}$. The lower priced bond's current yield is 7.33% as opposed to 7.12% for the other. Merely a few tenths of a percent, right? There are two significant implications involved here.

- First, on a purchase of 25 bonds you would have paid an **EXTRA $750 in commissions.**

- Second, and perhaps more important, if long-term interest

WHAT YOUR BROKER NEVER TELLS YOU

rates fall, the lower-priced bond will appreciate much faster, since it was priced fairly to begin with in relation to comparable long-term bonds. The higher priced bond will react slower because the extra $30 was artificially factored in by your friend, the broker. Moreover, the higher priced bond will **drop like a rock** if long-term rates rise simply because it was overpriced to begin with.

The sum and substance of bond trading is this: either pay the best price available or pay sticker... It's **YOUR** choice.

SUMMARY NOTE: It's important to grasp a salient point: choosing a firm is much less an investment factor than choosing a broker. If a broker is competent, honest, and makes money for you consistently, he can probably do it anywhere. Before you do any trading, be certain to use a seasoned broker, as he will probably be under less pressure in the brokerage house's ranking structure, and therefore less inclined to push the most profitable products in his firm's inventory - such as limited partnerships, tax shelters, and the like. Your innate loyalty is not the issue here - to a company, or your broker. Keep in mind that the **game** is all business. Friendships are extraneous to the process. As long as you are trading, you will be pampered and wooed. Let the commissions slow down and you will be treated like a jilted lover... ignored and forgotten.

WHAT YOUR BROKER NEVER TELLS YOU

How They Rank...

3rd **Client**

2nd **Broker**

1st **FIRM**

WHAT YOUR BROKER NEVER TELLS YOU

NEVER FORGET! Your interests come in a distant third behind the firm and the broker. Grasping this fact of life will serve to protect your money and once again help keep the playing field level.

CHAPTER FOUR
RESEARCH ANALYSTS

Gurus or Gophers?...

CHAPTER FOUR

Let's turn our attention to company analysts who serve in the research department of your brokerage house. Since research is broad in scope, it's useful to examine every aspect of the process, point by point. To begin, let's demonstrate the information funnel in its proper order: *See Fig. 7*

It should be common knowledge that giving or receiving inside information is illegal, and in a perfect world, such behavior would never happen. But look closely at the number of people involved in the **"information funnel graphic"**. Can you honestly believe that information **doesn't leak out** somewhere along the way? Remember, we are dealing with the **"what is"** and not what **"oughta be"**. By the time "information" finds its way to the analyst and he passes it along to the brokers in the firm, it's beyond "old news", it's downright stale. The "information" can take various forms, such as the announcement of a revolutionary new product line, record earnings far beyond the expectations of the Street, an impending takeover, a huge lawsuit that could prove devastating to earnings, or any number of other scenarios that could greatly affect the stock price, both up or down. Any big news invariably starts at the top of the information funnel and follows its way down.

Here's a couple of ways to test a stock's viability once it

The Information Funnel

Hypothetical N.Y.S.E. Company

Corporate Board Members
Senior Officers
Employees

Brokerage Firm's Research Dept.
Broker

Client

Figure 7

WHAT YOUR BROKER NEVER TELLS YOU

reaches the broker via an analyst in the firm:

- **First**, the next time you receive a **"hot tip"** from your broker, do a little homework and check to see what the stock price was 90 days ago.

A call to your local library can usually supply you with this information. If you find that the stock has risen significantly in price over the last three months, chances are it has already run its course *short term*. It is critical to remember that stocks are often bought on rumors and sold on news. I can recall dozens of occasions when a well-known stock was expected to announce great earnings at the end of the next quarter and accordingly, the stock price rose significantly in anticipation. When the earnings were announced and they were even **higher** than expected, the price **DROPPED**. Why? Because the expectations drove up the price more than the actual earnings did. Also, scores of people in the information stream knew how big the earnings were long before the announcement was ever made and were buying the stock. When the announcement was made, these same people were **SELLING, not buying!** Naturally, speculators always hope the news will be much better than expected, as if by some miracle, their ship will come in. Reality invariably leads to a let down: what we look forward to with avid interest is rarely as good as anticipated.

WHAT YOUR BROKER NEVER TELLS YOU

Conversely, if the price has been flat or even lower today than it was three months ago, you better have solid reasons for wanting to own it. An exception to these scenarios is that rare broker who has the ability to function as an analyst. He receives his information from outside sources and makes his own decisions, ignoring the inclination to follow the "herd". He seems to have a "feel" for identifying stocks overlooked by the other analysts on the Street. In other words, he has the perceptive instinct to spot the "sleepers". If he's given you credible information in the past which consistently makes money, stay with his ideas. He's a rare individual. This type of broker doesn't chase takeover or rumor stocks because he's learned that they usually don't pay off. Never forget that the market is nothing more that the collective thoughts of millions of people and usually serves as a bell weather to future economic events. In addition, it is also important to recognize that the market is a **"discounting mechanism"**. This means that it processes information and builds its findings into the stock price BEFORE any news gets out or any announcements are made. To grasp this notion, think back to a time when you heard about something new - such as the introduction of a new product, a breakthrough in medical research, a hot new toy, etc. You may have even considered buying shares of the stock. If you had checked its price 90 days earlier, you would have probably found that the stock had already made

WHAT YOUR BROKER NEVER TELLS YOU

its move by the time you're considering a purchase. Why? Because: by the time news of the product filtered down to you - either through your broker, a friend, or the media - the news had already reached the end of the information stream. Your broker is in almost the same situation as you. He is, at best, five steps removed from the original source of the information. That is why I strongly urge a **"backward look"** at any stock recommendation before you invest, regardless of where the "hot tip" originated.

- **Second,** keep a log of all the recommendations you receive and, by way of a chart, maintain a "fictitious" account. Use this to track the stocks performance assuming you did the **OPPOSITE** of what your broker recommended.

For example, if your broker recommends selling a stock you own, double-up on your position in the fictitious account by buying twice as much. If your broker recommends buying a stock, sell the position **"short"** in the bogus account. More often than not, you will find that going the opposite way of these supposedly "informed recommendations" will make money in high percentages. The reason is that stocks have an ebb and flow of their own. The time to "catch a wave" is BEFORE it starts to break, while it's still far from the shore, NOT when its lapping up on the beach. *See Fig. 8*

WHAT YOUR BROKER NEVER TELLS YOU

Time to Buy... Time to Sell

Time to Buy

Time to Sell

Shore

Figure 8

WHAT YOUR BROKER NEVER TELLS YOU

Using this analogy, the obvious time to buy a stock is NOT at the end of the information stream. If your timing is such that you are not early enough in the cycle to be buying, then perhaps you be thinking about selling... short-selling, that is. There are two sides to every transaction, remember?! For every buyer there is a seller. Short-sellers bet against the market, believing that it will drop. This is a more sophisticated approach to the market, but a viable one to select individuals. The results you find by doing this exercise will no doubt surprise you.

Anyone who believes that a broker has the **"inside track"** on information simply because of his proximity to the analysts is living in a Fool's Paradise. The investment business is a matter of **perception versus reality**. My clients would often joke about how much money I must be making in the market because I was so close to the "action". The reality was that I seldom made serious money trading for my own account. Moreover, I knew very few brokers who consistently made money in their own accounts, either. The lion's share of all our money came from commissions. Guess who supplied our daily bread?

- It is a historical fact that for 15 years, ending 1984, three quarters of professionally managed funds were unable to beat the Standard & Poor 500 Average.

WHAT YOUR BROKER NEVER TELLS YOU

To think that your broker is a transcendent economic guru is both naive and misguided.

Sage advice: be more reliant on outside opinions, those not affiliated with any brokerage house since they tend to be more objective. It's hardly a secret that the House (brokerage house) will carry large positions in many stocks held in their own account. You can be certain that it will not trash a stock in which it still carries a large position. If a certain stock situation changes and perhaps should be sold, you can't always be assured that you will be informed on a timely basis. As mentioned before, your interests are third in line behind the firm and the broker. If you consider such behavior a violation of you trust, your assumption would be on target. But that's irrelevant to the reality of the marketplace. Too often I have witnessed the results: Clients left holding the bag on a stock that should have been sold much earlier.

Before you make any decisions, it is important to weigh all the prevailing opinions against your own **"gut feeling"**. Here's a classic example that may stir up some memories: In the late 1970's, Chrysler stock sold for approximately $3 per share. The prevailing opinion was terribly negative. The firm I was with prohibited its brokers from soliciting purchase of the shares because it carried a "sell" opinion on Chrysler. At the time, I had been in the business a mere two years and was

WHAT YOUR BROKER NEVER TELLS YOU

certainly not Albert Einstein Jr., but I reasoned as follows:

Chrysler was in desperate straits and, in my humble opinion, had only three options…

- Declare bankruptcy;

- Agree to a buy out, i.e. merge with another company; or

- Accept the government loan bailout.

In my view, bankruptcy was not a likely scenario, especially since the political and economic ramifications were so overwhelming. Lee Iacocca played a major part of the equation. Pure reason suggested that other alternatives were much more probable. Of course there was risk - every stock carries with it an inherent risk. But when fear and panic rule the market and public opinion swings too far in one direction, the majority is usually wrong. Call it the **"Groth Law of Probability"**. When there is universal agreement on something, it's usually time to reverse course. This is the essence of contrarian thinking.

As you know, Chrysler - under the astute guidance of Mr. Iacocca - made an unbelievable comeback due, in part, to the government bailout. The company even repaid the loan early. Most brokerage firms, in their infinite wisdom, started recommending the stock for purchase around $25. Then

WHAT YOUR BROKER NEVER TELLS YOU

again, in all fairness, they **COULDN'T** have recommended the stock at $3. Why? Because the stakes were too high if they were wrong. If any broker in the firm were to solicit purchase of the stock and bankruptcy resulted, the attorneys of the clients involved would have had a field day in court. Naturally, any firm would defend its no-buy position, pleading it was safeguarding the best interests of its clients. But you, as a *PLAYER,* need to look past such a humanitarian facade and make choices that are best for YOU. The firm will **always** play the **CYA** (cover your a_ _) game. Its interests come first, remember? In that regard, the brokerage houses had no choice but to sit on the sidelines and wait for the outcome. The point is, you can't expect your broker to bring a **"cherry"** like this to the table. Many brokers I knew felt as I did that buying Chrysler stock at these low levels was a great play, but our hands were tied. As pointed out, when a firm has a "sell" opinion on a stock, brokers are prohibited from recommending it to their clients. All trades are monitored, and unless the order ticket is marked "unsolicited", the wire operator who sends the trade electronically to the floor of the exchange will send it back.

In other words, clients (or anyone for that matter) could call us and buy the stock but we could not call **them** and make a recommendation to buy it.

WHAT YOUR BROKER NEVER TELLS YOU

Ironically, scores of "buy" recommendations on other less risky stocks (touted as **"winners"** by the analysts) are pushed by the brokers everyday, losing money on a consistent basis. Again, it's a matter of whose agenda takes precedence. As you well know, Chrysler stock has profited far beyond anyone's wildest expectations since those scary days. Savvy investors who were willing to look beyond the hysteria and doom and gloom forecasts were picking up 1,000 share blocks at $3 for a paltry $3,000. By the time most firms were willing to start recommending the stock, the wily ones had made eight times their original investment! - with much more to come. The Chrysler comeback is a textbook example of how gut-level decisions can pay off. Intuition is sometimes a much better guide than an analyst's opinion.

Consider a more recent event: Black Monday, October, 1987. How many firms, or brokers for that matter, were suggesting buying stocks the day after that 500 point drop? Yet, within eighteen months, the market reached record highs. Remember the pendulum theory? In this case, negative sentiment had swung too far to one side. *See Fig. 9*

Please copy the following sentence for future reference:

- **At the point of highest fear and anxiety you will inevitably find the point of lowest risk.**

WHAT YOUR BROKER NEVER TELLS YOU

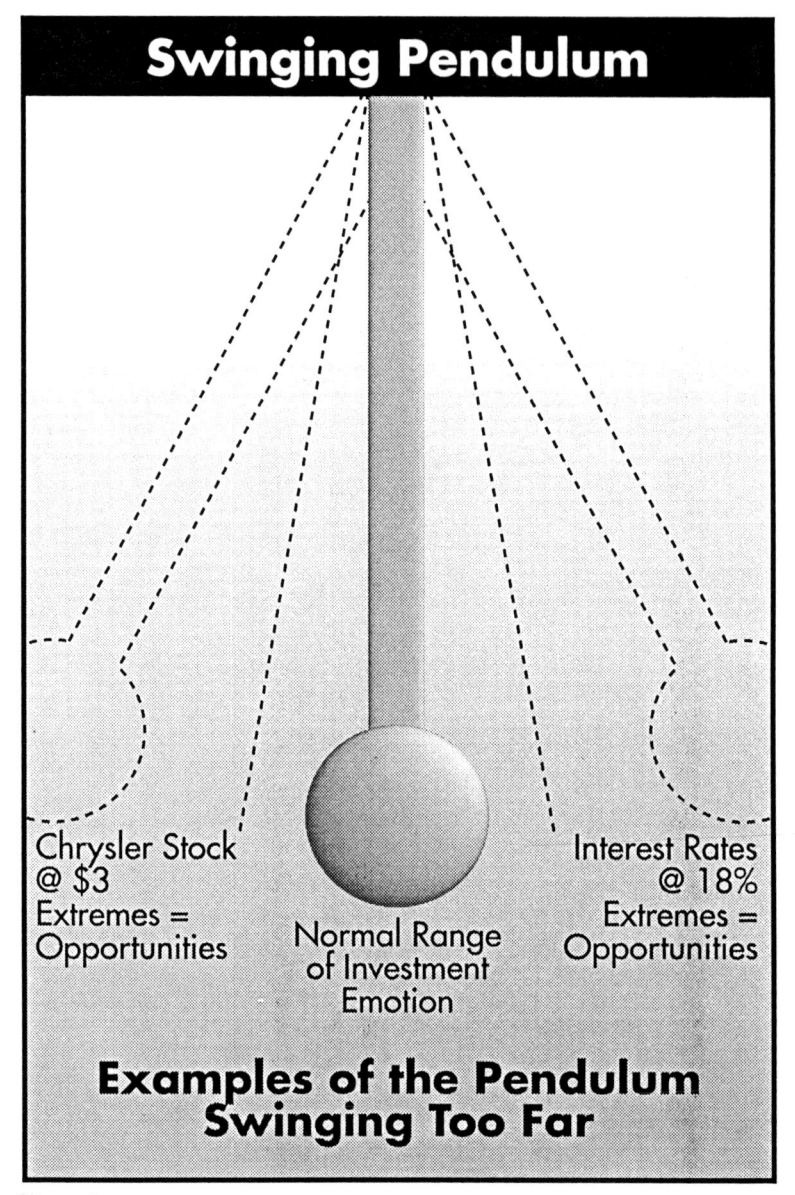

Swinging Pendulum

Chrysler Stock
@ $3
Extremes =
Opportunities

Normal Range
of Investment
Emotion

Interest Rates
@ 18%
Extremes =
Opportunities

Examples of the Pendulum Swinging Too Far

Figure 9

WHAT YOUR BROKER NEVER TELLS YOU

When fear is rampant, what are most people doing? You are CORRECT, sir - selling! So, at this point, the market is oversold and most of the risk has been wrung out of it. The same holds true in bull markets. If everyone is buying at a frenzied pace without regard for value, stocks become over-bought and, with fewer buyers around, the sellers enter the picture. During such times, logic and reason must prevail… but don't look to your broker to supply it. Put a premium on **YOUR** good sense and intuition.

SUMMARY NOTE: Don't be reticent about reevaluating your portfolio and asking common sense questions. The analysts aren't necessarily any better at picking stocks than you are! Their opinions are just that - opinions. Question everything. Seek outside sources, such as Value Line, Barrons, Standard & Poor, etc. A truism of the human race is that some individuals, motivated by the desire for money and power, will try to intimidate or otherwise influence you to buy into **their** own reasoning. Another common trait of human nature is a tendency to believe that all persons share noble thoughts and eschew ulterior motives. The headlines say otherwise. Never forget the simplest rule of business:

> **Whenever someone asks you to buy something, they have something to gain - ALWAYS.**

WHAT YOUR BROKER NEVER TELLS YOU

Your job is to evaluate the validity of the request and determine if it is mutually beneficial. Don't be awed by the image projected by brokers or analysts, who are neither Einstein's nor are they all good Samaritans. They are merely salespeople, driven by a desire to earn money - a compelling reason for you to maintain a watchdog attitude in any financial transaction. One final caveat: <u>*NEVER*</u> **TAKE YOUR EYES OFF YOUR CHIPS.**

CHAPTER FIVE
MANAGED ACCOUNTS

> *The Fairest Game In Town...*

CHAPTER FIVE

The stage is now set for the investor to play, as the title suggests, the fairest game in town. As we will see, having a managed account removes the broker's **conflict of interest**, as well as the firm's. For those of you unfamiliar with managed accounts, a professional portfolio (money) manager invests your funds on a discretionary basis. As mentioned in a previous chapter, this means that securities can be bought or sold at the discretion of the money manager - without consulting with you first. Thus, the name **discretionary account**. The benefit of this type of account is two fold.

- **First**, you don't have to be consulted every time a change in your account needs to be made.

- **Second**, since you are paying a flat fee for the service, you incur no transaction (commission) costs every time a trade is made.

The portfolio manager can buy and sell all he wants and you still pay **one fee**. You must sign a **discretionary account form** before any trading begins which gives him authority to act on your behalf. At the same time, however, you will supply him with a set of guidelines regarding what types of securities he can and cannot buy on your behalf. He has to operate within the parameters that you set.

WHAT YOUR BROKER NEVER TELLS YOU

In his book, *INVESTMENT POLICY: How To Win The Loser's Game*, Charles Ellis states

> "...clients of investment managers all too often delegate or more accurately abdicate to their investment managers responsibilities which they can and should keep for themselves. Their undelegatable responsibilities are: setting explicit investment policies consistent with their objectives, defining long-range objectives which are appropriate to their particular fund, and managing their managers to ensure that their policies are being followed."

For such expertise, you will be charged a percentage of your assets. The amount varies depending on the size of your account. Such charges, ranging from ½% to 3% annually, are normally assessed quarterly.

Since fees are settled up front and all parties have agreed to the terms, the conflict of interest is now removed from the equation. No more brokers agonizing as to whether he should buy or sell because it's the end of the month and he needs more commissions. The only consideration is market performance. Your **sole question** to the money manager at year-end should be:

> "Considering the fee I have paid you, how much has my portfolio grown this year?"

WHAT YOUR BROKER NEVER TELLS YOU

Commissions and trading patterns are now a moot point.

If you prefer to seek out your own money manager, it's possible to wire your funds or transfer assets directly to him, providing you meet his minimum account restrictions. If you don't feel comfortable choosing a manager, or are at a loss as to where to start, turn to your broker. He has access to hundreds of outside managers, as well as the firm's in-house manager. Sit down with your broker and evaluate your position. You should discuss with him, among other matters:

- Amount of funds/assets available
- Risk tolerance
- Investment objective
- Time lines
- Performance expectations

Using this information, your broker can now act as your agent, screening all the possible managers within the universe of those who fit your parameters. He should come back to you with a **"scatter gram"** showing all the possible choices that suit your profile. It should look something like this: *See Fig. 10*

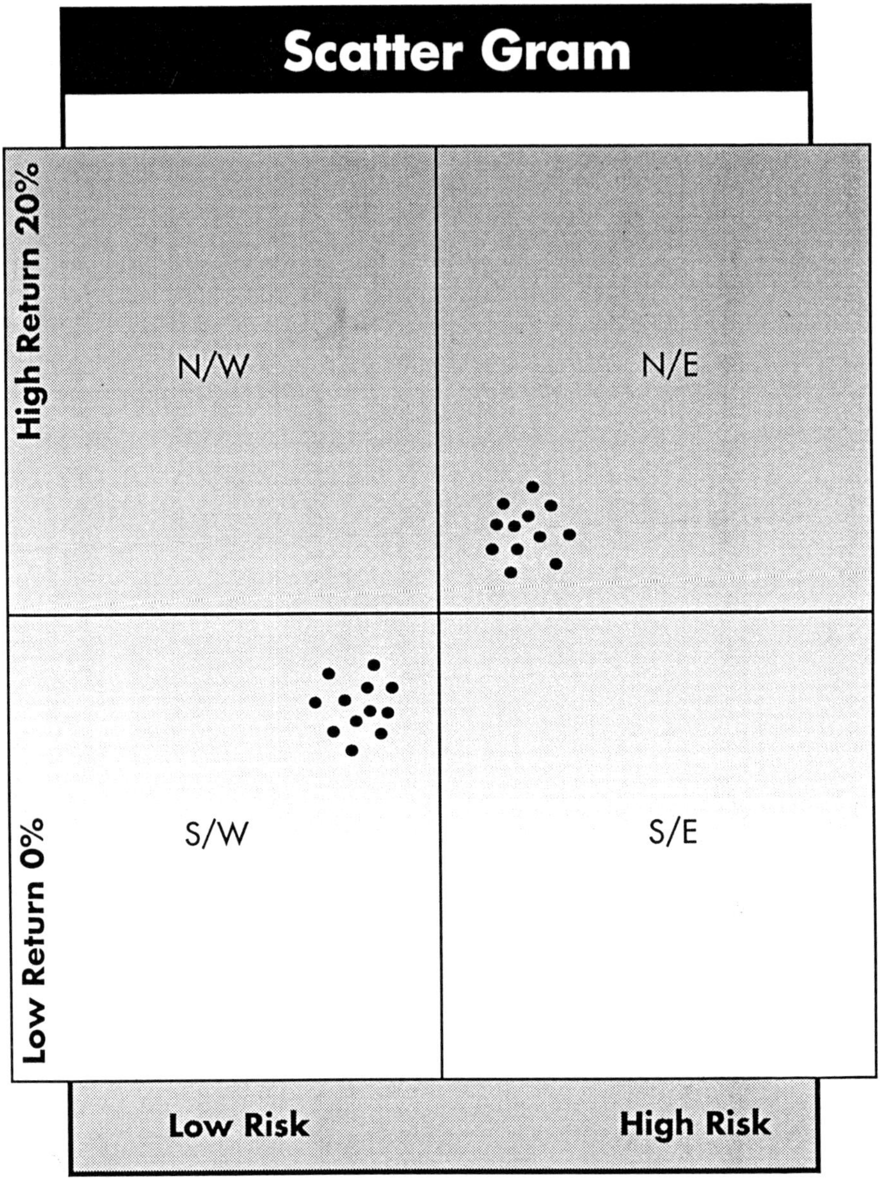

Scatter Gram

High Return 20% | **Low Return 0%**

N/W | N/E

S/W | S/E

Low Risk | **High Risk**

Figure 10

WHAT YOUR BROKER NEVER TELLS YOU

Let's take a look at the diagram. Someone looking for a high rate of return and is comfortable with greater risk would find his potential managers in the N/E quadrant. On the other hand, someone who is risk-aversive and willing to settle for a lower than average return in exchange for greater safety would find possible candidates in the S/W quadrant. From this narrowed list of managers you can now evaluate each manager separately, and select one whose background and investment philosophy closely matches your own.

Next, it's vital to compare your potential money managers investment performance over a one, five, and ten year period and compare it to the general market averages, such as the Dow Jones, S & P 500, etc. I would then check his performance against the other managers that fell within your quadrant. Consider also how he performs in bear markets, as well as bull markets. It's not very hard to make money when the market is always going up. It's infinitely harder, though, to hold your own when the markets are down. Your broker can supply all of this data. If your portfolio is large enough, you may choose to place your money with several managers to further diversify your assets. Another twist is to look at managers who are not too heavily burdened with an excessively large amount of assets under their control. Here's an analogy that illustrates the point: *See Fig. 11*

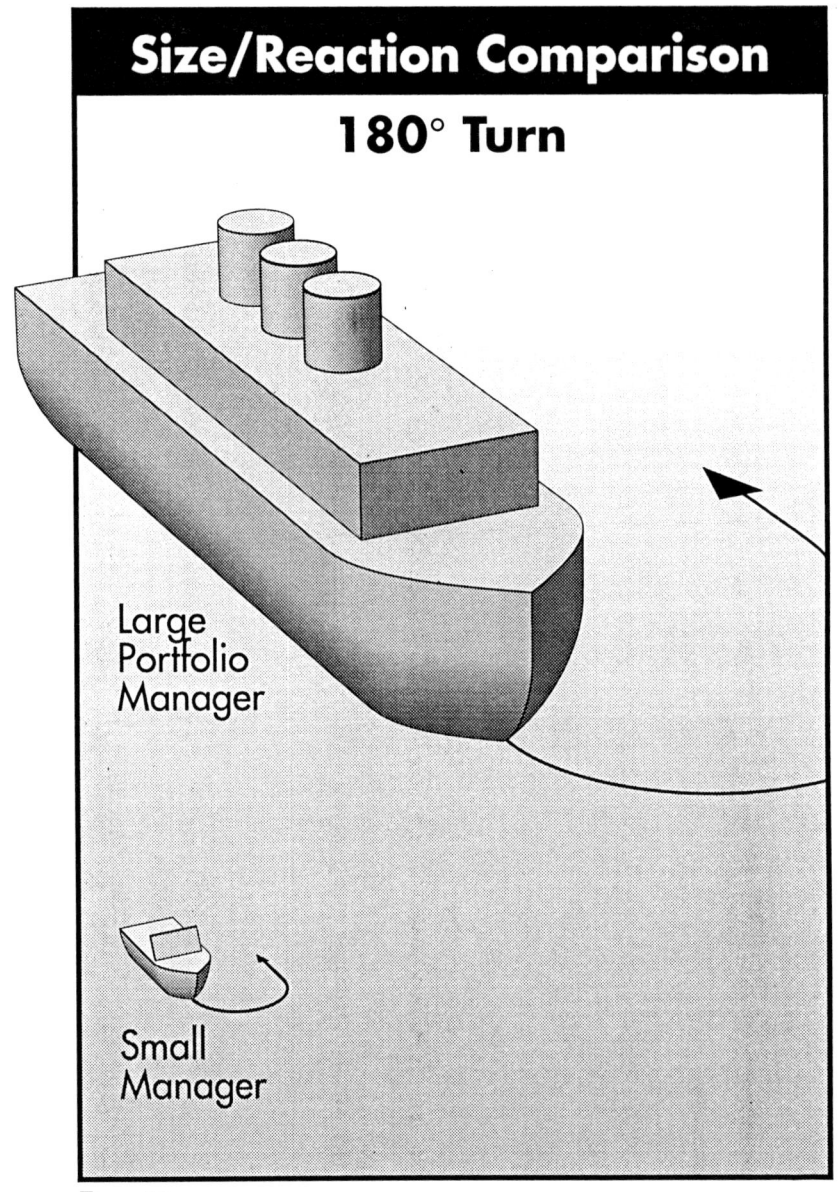

Figure 11

WHAT YOUR BROKER NEVER TELLS YOU

Imagine an ocean liner and a speedboat, both starting their turns simultaneously. One can maneuver 180 degrees in a few seconds while the bigger vessel requires a longer time frame simply because of its sheer size. By the same token, the smaller manager adapts to market changes very quickly while the larger manager will take longer to change positions. If the market turns south, the smaller manager can unload stocks immediately while the larger manager must lighten his positions incrementally so as not to cause a disruption on the trading floor. Too much stock put up for sale at one time could cause a panic. Another advantage of a smaller manager is that he can pick up shares of a thinly-floated stock (few shares available) which he believes is undervalued. These "small-capped" stocks can influence the return of the entire portfolio. By contrast, the larger manager either can't or won't buy these same shares because:

- There may not be enough shares available.

- Even if he could buy them, their scarcity would make the number of shares so small that it could not impact the portfolio simply because of its immense size.

Have you noticed throughout this discussion that your broker now wears a different **"hat"** and is sitting on YOUR side of the table? He is getting a piece of the management fee you're paying, so his compensation is taken care of. Now he can take care of **you**. You've taken him out of the role of "salesperson" and accorded him the role of **"consultant"**. His job is to help place your funds with an objective, third party. Your broker now acts as an intermediary between the portfolio manager and you. Accordingly, instead of digging for commissions, everyone is interested in one thing: **PERFORMANCE!** What a concept! Now, your broker is working *for you*, looking over the quarterly performance reports, evaluating the managers net return against similar managers within your investment parameters, etc. If your portfolio appears to be lagging in comparison to the general market averages or far below other, similar managers, he may suggest terminating the current manager and finding someone else to manage your funds. The bottom line with this strategy is that your broker is out of the picture with respect to choosing your investments.

One word of caution: don't be so results driven that you choose a different manager every year simply because someone else produced a better return. What is more important is the long-term consistency of results. If the manager's performance has been exemplary over a ten year period, one off year should not be a concern, providing nothing significant has changed, such as a major exodus of the top people, etc.

WHAT YOUR BROKER NEVER TELLS YOU

Other important factors are:

- How timely are the investment reports sent to you?

- How clear are they to understand?

- How accessible is the manager if you need to speak to him?

If you can answer these questions to your own satisfaction, and your **net** annual return is acceptable to you, then you have probably made a good choice.

One other advantage to using a money manager is that you've taken the **"performance monkey"** off your brokers back. This is no longer his responsibility, but that of the portfolio manager. Your broker simply shadows the manager to insure that he is doing HIS job, and not try to find new and creative ways to perform **"Commissiondectomies"** on you, à la Robert Ringer in **Winning Through Intimidation.**

For all the reasons mentioned, I believe that managed accounts are, indeed, the fairest game in town, not merely for the client, but for the broker as well. This is a situation in which everyone can win. The more seasoned and astute brokers are all placing as many qualified accounts under management as possible. In truth, this is a difficult transformation for a broker to make, since top producers can make significantly more money **"turning"** your investments over themselves, at least short-term. Commissions generated by your broker are paid to him every month. Big hitters are used to seeing fat commission checks roll in each month. Compare this to how managed accounts pay out. Remember, we mentioned the management fee is assessed quarterly against your account? That's when the manager and the broker get paid - when you pay them every 90 days. If you're a broker and are used to eating regularly, this is a long time between pay checks! On the other hand, those who have made the successful transition to managed account business will be infinitely better off in the long-run for several significant reasons:

- His image changes from a **"churn 'em and burn 'em"** broker to that of an advisor who works for your best interests.

- Since the burden of performance in now on the back of the money manager, there will be less incidence of disgruntled clients. If the performance isn't there, the manager is fired, not the broker.

- The pressure of generating commissions starts to slowly disappear simply because the compensation is "built-in" every three months.

WHAT YOUR BROKER NEVER TELLS YOU

But look closer: the manager's fee, and therefore the brokers cut, is based every year on the assets of the account. Assume for a moment that your account is growing at an average annual rate of 10%. This means that the manager and your broker will have a **built in raise** of 10% as well. Imagine a broker that has worked hard and now has $100 million under management. His yearly production (gross commissions) would probably be in the neighborhood of $1,500,000, giving him an annual income, at a 45% pay-out, of approximately $675,000 - which will grow every year at the same rate as the return on your assets. Now it may be easier to see why it is in your broker's best interest to serve you well, and **not** focus on commissions. If you're getting the return you hoped for, the compensation your broker earns is now irrelevant. In other words, you're **BOTH** getting what you want. If the portfolio manager and the broker both do their jobs well, the broker can walk in to work every January 1st and know that his income is fairly certain - and he never has to call you to make a trade! *See Fig. 12*

As the investor, you are now in the best position to win the game because your broker is now at your side serving as a watchdog over the money manager. Your interests are now being **protected instead of exploited**. Best of all is the fact that you're not paying a exorbitant fee for the service.

Portfolio Manager/Broker/Client

A Symbiotic Relationship

Figure 12

WHAT YOUR BROKER NEVER TELLS YOU

SUMMARY NOTE: For all the reasons stated above, a professionally managed account is a superior approach to the game. Remember that your goal should be to make money - **consistently**. No longer are you playing just to play.

So, you ask,

- "What does it take to engage a capable money manager?"

- "What constitutes a minimum account?"

The more well-known a portfolio manager is, the higher his minimum will be. You may find some minimums as low as $25,000, and many as high as $1 million or more. But rest assured, your broker will find a suitable manager with a minimum you will be able to meet. Once accomplished, you'll sleep easier and - thank heaven - not put up with any more hit and miss calls from your broker. Managed accounts are a much more defined investment approach. As with most endeavors, a well-thought-out plan of action will usually yield better results.

If you lack sufficient funds to meet a portfolio manager's minimum, using a mutual fund that meets your needs is the next best option. It may not be as tailored as you would like, but over time, your funds may grow to a point where you can now chose a manager. Follow he guidelines in that section to make your selection. Lastly, you may want to continue using your broker in the traditional sense following the guidelines recommended in this text. If you're doing well, there is no reason to be dissatisfied. At the same time, **knowing what your broker knows** will make you more confident in your decisions and no doubt enhance your overall return by cutting your transaction costs.

CHAPTER SIX QUESTIONS

You May Want To Ask...

CHAPTER SIX

WITH REGARD TO CHOOSING A BROKER:

Too often we assume that our broker is a wise, gifted soul with the sagacity of a Rhodes Scholar, the prophetic power of a Cassandra, and the earning capacity of Midas. But hold it! Let's make certain we know something about him **BEFORE** we turn over a dime. Here are a sampling of questions you should ask:

- How long have you been licensed?
- How would you describe your investment philosophy?
- What is your product mix?
- How would you describe your typical client?
- What is the average age of your clientele?
- Do you have any customer complaints on file?
- Do you restrict your accounts by a minimum size?
- What percentage of your business is managed by portfolio managers?
- What percentage of your business is institutional?

These questions are important because, if you're the

WHAT YOUR BROKER NEVER TELLS YOU

aggressive type and like to play the fast-paced index futures market, you'll be unhappy with an ultra-conservative Blue Chip stock-picker. If you're a young executive just starting to build a portfolio, and your broker handles predominately older persons with high net worths, you won't receive much attention. Your needs should match the style and temperament of the broker if you hope to have a successful relationship.

WITH REGARD TO STOCK PURCHASES:

- Does this stock recommendation fit my criteria?

- Who's pick is it: the broker's or the analyst's?

- Is this a rumor stock, one talked about in the Journal or Barrons as a take-over candidate?

- Are there strong fundamental reasons for me to own it?

- Does the stock have options in the event I want to cover my position?

- How are other stocks in this same group doing?

- What was the stock price 90 days ago?

- Will I have to liquidate one of my other holdings to finance the purchase of the new stock? Where is support on the stock, that point on the chart where bottoming usually occurs?

WITH REGARD TO STOCK SALES:

- When is the next ex-date, the date after which I would receive the my next quarterly dividend?

- Upon the sale of the stock, am I now being urged to buy something else?

- Where is resistance on the stock, that point on a chart where the stock usually tops out? Is it there yet?

- How is this stock performing compared to others in the same group? If they are all strong, selling now could be a mistake.

- What (or who) is leading me to decide on selling at this particular time?

- Could I sell a call option (cover my position) against the stock to increase its yield?

- Could I use a stop-loss order to protect the downside?

Amazingly, a large number of investors don't consider any of the above factors in their investment planning. You can't **assume** that your broker will call these to your attention, either.

WHAT YOUR BROKER NEVER TELLS YOU

A BRIEF OVERVIEW...

I've mentioned several times that covered option writing as an excellent strategy to increase the yield on your portfolio. For those who aren't familiar with this investment tool, I'll try to explain it as simply and clearly as possible. Please note: in order to employ this strategy, you must have **signed option papers on file** before you start trading.

There are speculators in the market who are willing to "**bet**" that certain stocks will rise or fall within a certain time frame. They assume 100% risk, which means that if they are wrong, they can lose it all. These speculators trade stock options on the various exchanges, such as the CBOE (Chicago Board Options Exchange). Here is an example of how it works:

Suppose you own a stock that is **"optionable"** (not all stocks are) and currently is trading a $33 per share. A speculator (the **option buyer**) would pay you (the **option seller**) a specific sum of money (called the **premium**) to buy your stock from you at $40 *IF* the stock price is $40 or more by the third Friday of the expiration month. If the stock is at $40 or above on expiration day, you MUST sell the stock is it's called, regardless of how high it might be. To know how much a speculator might pay you, simply look in the financial section of the newspaper under the options section and find the stock, strike price (in this case, $40), and the expira-

WHAT YOUR BROKER NEVER TELLS YOU

tion month you wish. You will find that there are various expiration months and strike prices to choose from. Each day, the options prices will change because these prices reflect the underlying stock price. Translated, this means that if the stock price goes up or down, so goes the option price.

Given the previous example, if the stock price on expiration was $42, your stock would be **"called away"** at $40, and your profit would be your original cost basis plus the option premium minus $40. If the stock is under $40 on the expiration date, you keep the stock **PLUS** the option premium **PLUS** any dividends paid and can then turn around and **do it again**.

- This strategy can conservatively add **5-10%** per year to your portfolio - and best of all - you assume **no risk of loss!**

The option buyer assumes all the market risk. The "risk" you assume is **opportunity risk**, the possibility that your stock could rise higher than the strike price, denying you further opportunity to participate. The following illustration may help: *See Fig. 13*

The **only** decision that you have to make is whether or not you would be willing to sell your stock at a specific, predetermined time and price. Selling the option against your stock is

Covered Option Scenario

Expiration Day

Strike Price $40

$33 Purchase Price

3rd Friday of Expiration Month:

Stock price $40 or more: stock almost always called away. You Keep: • Profit (including option premium) • Any Dividends Paid	Stock price under $40: You Keep: • Stock • Any Dividends Paid • Option Premium • Repeat Process

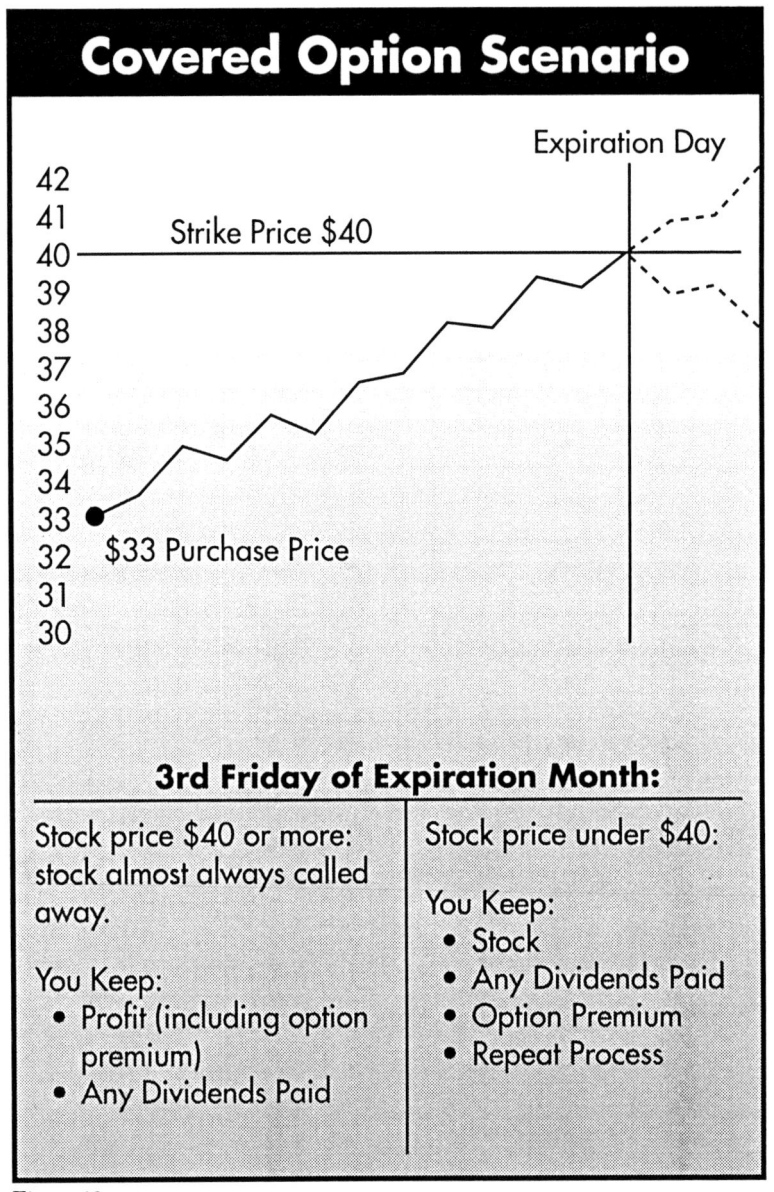

Figure 13

called **"covered option writing"**. If, after covering your position, the stock starts to climb near your strike price and you're now having second thoughts about it being called away, you can always buy back the option and **"roll-out"** to the next expiration month and strike. There are many option strategies, such as combos, straddles, shorts, going "naked", "lifting a leg", bull spreads, bear spreads, etc., that are too complicated to discuss here, but at least you will recognize the jargon when you hear it.

I realize that all of this sounds terribly complicated, but it's not as bad as you think. For further clarification of options trading, talk to your broker or pick up a book at the library.

One final note: I went into detail about options because many brokers don't like to cover stocks simply because, unless you buy back the option back early, you're locked in until the expiration date. This could prevent the broker from suggesting you sell when HE needs the commission. On the other hand, the brokers that have covered stocks for their clients wait anxiously for expiration dates, hoping that the stock is over the strike price and gets called away - generating another commission and freeing-up new money for investment.

WHAT YOUR BROKER NEVER TELLS YOU

Then there's always the broker who can't wait for the expiration date and starts to get creative...

Follow me closely on this one: I saw the actual client holding pages in question (every trade a broker makes is recorded on this document), so what I'm reporting is first hand. This particular broker would turn a **four commission scam** as follows:

1) Buy a stock... 1st <u>commission</u>

2) Cover the stock (sell option)... 2nd <u>commission</u> wait a few weeks

3) Buy back the option... 3rd <u>commission</u>

4) Sell the stock... 4th <u>commission</u>

Then repeat the process with a new stock, **over and over and over... Is** this excessive? Not if you're into bondage and pain! This is a case in point where the investor HAS to monitor his own account and look for inconsistencies, **EVEN** if the broker tells you that this is a good deal. Simply look at the trades, adding up the purchases and subtracting the sales. If the net result is a negative, you know something smells. People can lie; the numbers won't.

WHAT YOUR BROKER NEVER TELLS YOU

WITH REGARD TO CORPORATE BONDS:

- Is the bond listed?

- How is it rated?

- Is it selling at a **premium or a discount**? (over or under $1000)

- If it's selling at a premium and **callable**, how close is it to the call date?

- If it's called early, what would be the yield-to-call? Would I incur a capital loss?

- Are the interest payments adequately covered by the issuing corporation? (à la the junk bond fiasco)

- Am I buying for income or long-term appreciation?

- What is my time frame for holding the bond?

- What is my "gut feeling" versus the general consensus about which direction interest rates are headed?

To get the best prices, I would suggest buying only **listed bonds**. There are three important reasons for this:

1) The prices are auctioned on the bond exchange, similar to stocks, assuring the best market price.

WHAT YOUR BROKER NEVER TELLS YOU

2) You can check the prices daily in the paper without calling your broker to get a bid from the trader.

3) The commissions on listed bonds are fairly uniform from firm to firm; this eliminates excessive mark-ups.

If your broker does suggest a non-listed bond that sounds attractive, follow the guidelines in Chapter Two to safeguard against over-paying. It's critical to look carefully at interest rates before you buy. If rates are historically high, as they were in the 1980's, you can profit tremendously. If rates are at the low end of the cycle, don't expect much appreciation, because if rates go up, as they inevitably do, your bonds will fall in value.

Be wary of lower rated bonds, known as junk bonds, that could be in jeopardy of not being able to make the interest payments. Corporations that run into cash-flow problems can decide to cut or eliminate the dividend on stocks, but when they can't meet the interest payment on a bond, they are, by definition, insolvent. When this happens, not only do you forfeit your interest payments, but the price of the bond plummets.

I have omitted **municipal bonds** in this discussion for several reasons:

- The interest is tax-exempt from federal, and possibly, state and city tax, and;

- As a rule, these are not trading vehicles.

Typically, investors buy municipal bonds for the tax-exempt income they derive from them. To trade them would mean possibly losing an attractive tax-exempt interest rate, as well as incurring a possible capital gain on the trade, which is a taxable event. The two philosophies just don't mix. Muni bond prices react inversely to interest rates just like corporates, and as with any bond issue, carefully consider the revenue source that will fund the interest payments.

WITH REGARD TO BOND UNIT INVESTMENT TRUSTS:

- Is the trust I'm considering a new offering or one on the secondary market?

- Is the trust selling at a premium or a discount?

- How are the bonds rated?

- What is the average life of the trust, or the remaining life in the case of a secondary issue?

By way of explanation, a closed-end unit trust is a group of bonds, either corporate or municipal, that are placed into a trust and held there until every bond is matured or called away, pursuant to a call provision. In other words, it has a finite life. Compare this to a bond mutual fund, in which the fund manager can buy and sell bonds within the fund and it can, literally, run forever. A unit trust, by contrast, has no fund manager because there isn't anything to manage. Once the trust is set in place, each of the bonds in the trust matures according to its terms and the trust becomes **self-liquidating**. When the last bond in the trust matures, the trust ceases to exist.

Unit trusts definitely have a place in the proper portfolio. They are appealing because they can be bought in one-unit increments (approximately $1,000), and their interest is paid **monthly**, an attractive feature for those who are looking for consistent monthly income. There are two **caveats** to keep in mind when considering the purchase of unit investment trusts.

- **First**, new offerings in some firms can take almost **three months** to make a full interest payment, since it takes that amount of time for the pool of bonds in the trust to generate enough income to make the first payment.

- **Second**, many bonds in the trust will be at a **premium** to help keep the unit trust interest rate high. As call dates come up on the various bonds, they will be redeemed at par. Not only will your monthly interest go down (there are now less bonds available to contribute to the interest pool), but you will incur a capital loss on those bonds bought at a premium. In other words, let's assume that one of the bonds in the trust was selling at $1,100 when it was placed into the trust. If a call date comes up enabling the issuing corporation to call in the bond at $1,000 before maturity, then you would sustain a $100 capital loss, as well as losing the income that the bond generated.

My **best advice**, in most cases, is to buy unit trusts in the **secondary market**. Every unit trust starts out as a new offering to the public. As these new buyers need to sell the trust for any reason, the brokerage firm buys it back and **"makes a market"** for the security, holding it in inventory. Everyday an inventory sheet is circulated to the brokers so that they can see what is available to offer to their clients. This inventory sheet will show how many units of a particular trust are available, price per unit, current yield, yield to maturity, years left in the trust, etc. Any trust with a price over $1,000 per unit is selling at a premium and is subject to an early call of the bonds, as mentioned earlier. So, be advised. Every trust is required to have an accompanying

WHAT YOUR BROKER NEVER TELLS YOU

prospectus which will identify each bond in the trust, its bond rating, call provisions, etc.

Remember that these are **non-listed securities** and won't be found in the financial section of the newspaper. Most brokers love to sell these investments because the **mark-up** is generous, and the **pay-out is higher** because it is an **in-house** product. As mentioned earlier in the book, any product initiated by the firm, such as its own mutual funds, unit trusts, and tax shelters, etc., will pay the broker a richer pay out because **all** the money stays within the firm. Most brokerage houses carry huge inventories of unit trusts, so finding one to fit your needs shouldn't be too difficult.

A major benefit of a secondary trust is that is pays its **monthly interest payment immediately,** unlike the 90 day waiting period for some new offerings. In my experience I found that immediately after buying a trust on the **offering**, the price fell. Choosing a trust on the secondary market gives it a chance to adjust to market conditions, thereby offering better prices, which in turn gives better yields. Buying a trust on the offering is analogous to buying a new car, driving it off the lot, around the block, and back to the dealer, only to find that the price just **dropped $5,000. BE ADVISED:** All products can vary from firm to firm. Some firms restructure the sales charge and amortize it over a period of time so that the new offering **doesn't drop** in value right away and it's the secondary offering that becomes less attractive. You have to know what questions to ask, such as:

- How is the sales charge treated?

- Which trust - new or secondary - gives me the greatest benefit?

Be leery of **high-yield trusts**. While they function in the same manner as a standard trust, they are loaded with junk bonds to assure an unusually high yield. Naturally, such trusts appeal to unsuspecting investors, but it's wise to remember that surface attraction - like the top of an ocean wave - may hide the rocks below. Never take anything for granted or believe everything you hear, even if it's from your trusted broker. As the saying goes, "If it sounds too good to be true, it probably is". Think about it: If prevailing long-term bond rates are at 8%, and you hear of a trust paying 11%, ask yourself:

> **"How can this be?" The answer, of course, is: it can't be - not without assuming higher risk!**

Let me illustrate this point with a true story that you may find hard to believe. I assure you it happened.

WHAT YOUR BROKER NEVER TELLS YOU

I was working with a broker who, at that time had eight years experience and was one of the highest producers in the firm, earning almost $200,000 per year. Although a school teacher before becoming a broker, this person had great sales ability. Incredibly, this broker **sold millions** of dollars of high-yield **(JUNK)** unit investment trusts to clients **without the slightest knowledge** that these were **high-risk investments!** The poor fool wasn't even AWARE of the risks associated with these trusts, while the clients weren't aware of what they were buying! The only thing that mattered was the high interest rate because it was an easy sale. So what happened to the broker? Did this person get fired or reprimanded? No on both counts. The frightening aspect about this is that the majority of the clients never knew what happened! Believe it or not, short of outright breaking the law, brokers won't get into hot water for this sort of practice. Product ignorance within the industry is so widespread that it's almost impossible to police by management.

> **The unwritten rule is this:** Generate enough commissions to the brokerage house and almost **ANYTHING** can be swept under the carpet.

I've seen it happen over and over again. If a client files a complaint or initiates a lawsuit against the broker, the firm will simply, quietly settle the complaint by paying off the

WHAT YOUR BROKER NEVER TELLS YOU

client while the broker goes on cranking out more commissions. Some of what I've seen is astounding. Could the clients mentioned in the above story have found out what happened? Of course. All they had to do was look in the prospectus they received and checked the bond ratings. In reality, most, if any, did not.

Remember the story in an earlier chapter about the broker that was buying investments and sticking them into unsuspecting clients accounts? This same broker was getting almost **one complaint PER WEEK** from angry clients who were catching on to his scams. The manager simply kept settling the cases under the table and it was business as usual.

Something else you need to be made aware of…

Many firms, the ones I worked for included, will let clients **"swap"** unit trusts for tax reasons and give the investor a big break on the commissions, since they are merely trading one trust for another. This means that you could sell one of your existing trusts for a tax loss and replace it with a similar trust and realize the tax savings, without losing the income… as long as your friend, the broker, stipulates on the order that this is an **exchange**. If he doesn't, and **TWO order tickets** are entered, one ticket for the sale and another for the new purchase, guess what? You still realize the tax savings, but you pay full-boat commissions all over again! You might ask yourself why a broker wouldn't mark the trade an exchange and give you the commission break. Simple:

- **If you <u>pay a smaller commission</u>, the broker <u>receives a smaller commission</u>.**

Alas, it's always a money issue. This also means that you are now paying a higher price for the new trust and consequently earning a lower yield. How would you know? **YOU WOULDN'T!** This is a net trade, remember... no commissions are evidenced on the confirmation statement! I saw a friend of mine **"stick it"** to a client by doing this, knowing full well that she could have saved the client quite a few dollars; but alas, it was the end of the month... and you already know the rest.

IN SELECTING A MONEY MANAGER:

- Where did he get his experience?

- How long has he been a portfolio manager?

- Who are some of his corporate clients?

- Is he conservative or more aggressive?

- What is his minimum account size?

WHAT YOUR BROKER NEVER TELLS YOU

- How is his performance in good markets? Bad Markets?

- How easy to read are the quarterly and year-end statements?

- If applicable, how long has your broker used him as a manager?

- How accessible is the manager if I have questions?

In choosing a money manager, be honest with yourself in terms of **what you really want**, not **what you THINK you want**. When investors hear reports of managers with 20% returns, excitement reigns and they want in on the action. In truth, such investors are usually risk-aversive and likely to lose sleep with nagging worry about the safety of their money. The fact is, you will **not** realize a 20% return without assuming **considerable risk**. Accept that as an enduring warning. Check the scatter-gram in Chapter Four. Low risk investments yield low return and a higher measure of safety. High-risk investments only give you the possibility of greater returns. Before you invest a dime, be sure to know the measure of your risk-tolerance or you're bound to be disappointed - and sleepless.

CONCLUSION...

I began this writing by stating that **"broker bashing"** was not my intent. It remains my goal. I am not opposed to anyone trying to make a good living. The more accomplished a person is at his job, the more money that person is entitled to make. On the other hand, that does **NOT** mean that you, as a client, should pay more for a service than is necessary. In any profession, one can always make a substantial income without subterfuge, unnecessary fees, or other questionable practices. As we've seen with managed accounts, a broker can make an extraordinary living while still providing a needed service at a fair price. Above all, the compelling factors in playing the game successfully are:

- Understanding the markets as best you can
- Knowledge of your broker's background and capabilities
- A willingness to accept responsibility for whatever happens.

It's **YOUR** money! Watch it the same way you would guard your *wallet* if you rode the subway after dark! Understanding the **game** and its **rules** should enable you to become a more knowledgeable and skillful player.

WHAT YOUR BROKER NEVER TELLS YOU

My hope is that this book has given you a new insight as to how the system works. It is not perfect, but armed with the specific knowledge you have gained by reading the contents of this book, you can use it to your advantage. It is also my sincere wish that the information contained herein will allow you to prosper as never before. Be happy, always play to win, and *never, NEVER* **take your eyes off your chips!**

WHAT YOUR BROKER NEVER TELLS YOU

Glossary of Terms

GLOSSARY

ACCRUED INTEREST
Interest earned on a bond since the last interest payment, prorated daily.

ASSET ALLOCATION
How assets are diversified between various investments; stocks, bonds, real estate, etc.

ASSETS UNDER MANAGEMENT
Those securities managed by a broker, portfolio manager, or other financial advisor.

BOND RATINGS
Major rating services that evaluate the financial strength of a company. From highest to lowest: AAA, AA, A, BBB, BB, B, CCC, CC, C.

BREAK-OUT
Technical point on a chart at which the security breaks through the area where it usually topped out and began to retrace.

BREAK POINTS
Dollar amount levels at which the commission (sales) charge goes progressively lower.

CALLED AWAY
Stock taken (sold) away from option seller because stock was at or above the strike price on the 3rd Friday of the expiration month.

CALL FEATURE
Early redemption date of a bond prior to maturity at par.

WHAT YOUR BROKER NEVER TELLS YOU

CALL OPTION
Right of option buyer to buy 100 shares of stock at specified time and price from option seller.

CORPORATE BOND
Interest-bearing promissory note issued by a corporation with a stated rate of interest and maturity date.

COUPON
That part of a bond stating the rate of interest to be paid.

COVERED CALL WRITING
Also known as covering a position. Stockholder sells one call option per 100 shares of stock, agreeing to sell the stock if it reaches a specified price by a specified date.

CURRENT YIELD
Annual bond interest/stock dividend divided by the current bond/stock price.

DISCOUNT
Amount of a bond selling below par, usually $1,000; or a reduced amount given on commission charges.

DISCRETIONARY ACCOUNT
Written approval by investor giving money manager right to buy/sell securities at his discretion, without prior contact, as long as established parameters are followed.

EXCHANGE
Place where securities are traded, i.e., New York Stock Exchange, American Exchange, Midwest Exchange, etc.

WHAT YOUR BROKER NEVER TELLS YOU

EX-DATE
Date after which stock purchaser is not entitled to the current quarterly dividend.

GOVERNMENT BOND
Promissory note backed by the full faith and credit of the U.S. Government.

HIGH-YIELD UNIT INVESTMENT TRUST
Corporate/municipal bonds in trust with ratings of BB or lower.

IN-HOUSE FUNDS
Mutual fund managed by the brokerage house offering it.

IN-HOUSE MANAGER
Portfolio manager working for the brokerage firm.

JUNK BONDS
Speculative corporate bonds with a debt rating of BB or lower.

MAKING A MARKET
Brokerage house keeps securities in its inventory for sale or purchase as opposed to securities that are listed on an exchange.

MUNICIPAL BONDS
Promissory notes issued by state, city, county, or state authority that offer tax-exempt interest.

NON-DISCRETIONARY ACCOUNT
Client must give consent for any purchase or sale before the trade is made, either in person or by phone.

WHAT YOUR BROKER NEVER TELLS YOU

NON-LISTED PRODUCTS
Securities not traded on the major exchanges, but held in the brokerage firm's inventory.

PAR
Maturity price of a bond, usually $1,000.

PAY OUT
Percentage of gross commissions (production) that broker receives as income.

POINTS
Gross commission paid to broker on fixed-income products; one point usually equals $10.

PORTFOLIO MANAGER
Professional money manager who decides asset allocation and securities selection within the portfolio; usually works on fee basis or percentage of assets.

POSITION
Investment stake in a security.

PRODUCTION
Gross commissions generated to the firm by the broker.

PROPRIETARY PRODUCTS
In house securities; all revenue stays within firm.

WHAT YOUR BROKER NEVER TELLS YOU

PROSPECTUS
Formal, written proposal to sell securities; outlines facts necessary for investor to make a decision.

PREMIUM
Amount of a bond selling over par; or the cost of an option.

PUT OPTION
Right to sell 100 shares of underlying stock at specified price and time.

RESISTANCE
Price at which there is more supply than demand; stock usually "tops out" due to more sellers than buyers. Going through resistance is called a "break out".

ROLLING OUT
Buying back the existing covered option (closing the position) and re-writing with a different expiration date and strike price.

ROUND TRIP
Paying a commission on a buy/sell trade.

SECONDARY ISSUE
After initial offering to public, security held in inventory of member firm where it makes a market.

SHORT SALE
Investor borrows stock from brokerage house to sell with hopes of repurchasing at a lower price for a profit.

WHAT YOUR BROKER NEVER TELLS YOU

STOP-LOSS ORDER
Sell order placed on a stock below the current market price; if stock price falls below this price, it automatically becomes an open order to sell "at the market" to prevent further loss.

STRIKE PRICE
Predetermined price at which covered stock must be sold if exceeded by the 3rd Friday of the expiration month.

SUPPORT
Price at which there is more demand than supply; stock usually bottoms out due to more buyers than sellers.

THIN FLOAT
Small number of shares available for purchase or sale on the market.

UNIT INVESTMENT TRUST
Fixed portfolio of income producing securities held until maturity. A self liquidating investment with a finite life.

YIELD TO CALL
Return on investment figured to first call date.

YIELD TO MATURITY
Return on investment if held to maturity.